Innoliteracy™

Innoliteracy™

From Design Thinking to Tangible Change

Steinar Valade-Amland

First published in 2018 by
Business Expert Press, LLC
222 East 46th Street, New York, NY 10017
www.businessexpertpress.com

ISBN-13: 978-1-94784-370-7 (paperback)
ISBN-13: 978-1-94784-371-4 (e-book)

Business Expert Press Portfolio and Project Management Collection

Collection ISSN: 2156-8189 (print)
Collection ISSN: 2156-8200 (electronic)

Peer reviewed and originally published by DJØF Publishing, Copenhagen under the title "INNOLITERACY – fra design thinking til håndgribelig forandring" – ISBN9788757434941

Cover and interior design by S4Carlisle Publishing Services Chennai, India
Illustration art work: Morten U. Petersen, Reflekt Design, Copenhagen

First edition: 2018

10 9 8 7 6 5 4 3 2 1

Printed in the United States of America.

Abstract

INNOLITERACY™ – *From Design Thinking to Tangible Change* encourages reflection and inspires you to embark on your next development or change project. Taking its flight from the idea that all change for the better –whether constituted by something entirely new or an improvement of something already existing – is innovation; the author takes us on a journey of all the considerations one ought to keep in mind before solving a problem or addressing a challenge. The overall message of the book is to allocate much more resources to the earliest phases of a project – to the fuzzy front end, where the problem is unveiled and understood, defined and challenged, and where the roadmap for how to replace the existing with something better is drawn.

These ideas are depicted in a process model inspired both by well-known, linear stage-gate models and design methodological and often much more organic models – merged into a process, where each singular element can be opted in or out, depending on the project. Its intention is not to replace, but rather, add a layer of considerations, which may strengthen and enhance the models or processes you already use. By applying some of the thinking presented in the book, it is quite likely that your development and change project will be just as efficient as they are today, but with more focus on reflection and framing, scoping and reframing, stakeholder engagement and prototyping – helping you to achieve the best possible end result.

INNOLITERACY talks to everyone who works with or has the overall responsibility for – even those who are just curious about – change and development processes, especially on how they are made more stakeholder-focused and how one makes sure that the real problem is addressed. And by spending time up-front to identify the most relevant problem to solve, the risk of the solution failing to resonate with its audience is minimized. The book is a series of reflections, experiences, observations, and anecdotes on the one hand and a guide to a better development process on the other, also referring to examples and case studies in addition to literature and research. Its mission is to inspire more meaningful and thoroughly framed problem solving to benefit us all, to allow for more reflection, both individually and as teams, and to make sure that we exploit all the knowledge and experience that we have direct access to, just by choosing a more inclusive and open innovation process.

Keywords

creativity, creative culture, cyclic and iterative, fuzzy front-end, Innovation, prototyping, reflection, risk management, stakeholder engagement, user-centered

Contents

Foreword

Our time is rich in complex problems. Regardless of whether they are faced by the private sector CEO experiencing new technologies undermining current business models or by the public sector leader failing to create change for her citizens, matching her hopes and aspirations, they both search for adequate approaches and methods, which can help them navigate and reach their goals amidst a complex and turbulent reality.

Steinar Valade-Amland acknowledges in *INNOLITERACY* that our time is also rich in management literature claiming to offer the right answers. A rapidly growing and barely transparent fan of propositions claims to offer exactly what it is that the modern leader needs to create the needed results, despite whatever difficult context he finds himself in. Most often, the method comes first – then the problem has to be molded to fit in.

The possibly most valuable contribution of *INNOLITERACY* is that the author persists in putting the problem – and the reflections needed to understand it – first. This in itself is not new; one of my predecessors at Danish Design Centre, Jens Bernsen,[1] published his book entitled *The Problem Comes First*, making the same point nearly 25 years ago. However, what is new is the focus on the ability to reflect and the genuine curiosity of the leader, as Steinar Valade-Amland does in his book. And – as a natural consequence hereof – acknowledge that the key lies in identifying the "right problem," and thereafter, the right set of methods to address and solve it.

The American philosopher John Dewey[2] once wrote that the acknowledgment of the fact, the first step toward resolving a problem, is genuine curiosity and an urge to research. The design methods and

---

[1] J. Bernsen. (1989). *Design – The Problem Comes First* (Copenhagen, Denmark: Danish Design Centre).
[2] J. Dewey. (1938). *Logic: The Theory Of inquiry* (New York, NY: Henry Holt and Company).

approaches described by Valade-Amland in INNOLITERACY lean closely up against John Dewey's insistent claim that thinking and doing cannot be seen as independent processes, but only as each other's pre-requisites. Only through the creation of prototypes and user testing – iteration after iteration – the hypotheses and the framing of the problem are validated. The very specific approach of designers simply contributes to translate abstract notions of a problem, ideas, and concepts into tangible representations of form and material, and of an aesthetic that people can interact with. When the context is complex and the problems are wicked, this iterative approach involving real human beings, systems, and organizations is the only one way that new knowledge and insights is acquired.

Thus, the ability to make one's way toward new knowledge, learning, and reflections becomes a central element in fostering innovation and change in organizations. My experience is that it also requires a combination of courage, patience, and genuine curiosity to allow for the space and time for true reflection. If anything at all is under pressure in our time, it is the space – and the pauses – to cater to what is needed from organizations, leaders, and development staff. We lack both the systemic and the more random facilitation of reflection and of acquiring insights. Demands of performance, new digital media, and our organizational structures simply do not allow for the space needed to foster true innovation. It is my hope that the readers of *INNOLITERACY* will acknowledge how important prerequisites of space for reflection is to succeed at fostering the changes for the better world that we all dream of.

Christian Bason[3], PhD
CEO, *Danish Design Centre*

---

[3] Author of "Leading Public Sector Innovation" (2010), "Velfærdsinnovation (Welfare Innovation)" (2010), "Design for Policy" (2014), "Form Fremtiden (Form the Future)" (2016), "Leading Public Design" (2017).

Preface

Only God knows how many more or less patronizing management books are published annually, bringing more or less useful knowledge and insights to the market. So many, that it feels quite intimidating adding yet another title to the shelves. When, in spite of this observation, deciding to spend valuable time on writing down my own reflections on how to spur innovation and improve the chances that the outcome resonates with whomever the innovation was intended to move, it can only be explained by an urge to share my own experiences and ideas based on more than two decades of working with the development of strategies for products and services, organizations and business models, brand identities, and communication. I have seen how many common denominators there are between these different development processes, and how their outcomes are directly related to the combination of one's choice of methodology and the underlying motives and mind-sets.

This book reaches out to all companies, organizations, institutions, and authorities – leaving little behind – which, over and over again, experiences that their products, services, initiatives, and campaigns are not received with salute. Not as an exhaustive recipe for how or what to do, but hopefully, as a source of inspiration to gradually adopt some of the ideas and some of the mind-set, some of the techniques, and some of the methodologies described as we move along the process.

During most of my professional career, I have worked with and for design and designers, thus following the methodological progress and discourse intimately. The domain and identity of design have gradually moved away from its roots in arts and crafts – focusing on aesthetics, form, and function – toward an almost transversal approach to solving problems and to the development of new and the improvement of existing products and services, communication, and experiences, relations, and business models. One of my observations has been, and still tends to be, that design as methodology – despite overwhelming documentation of design's indisputably positive effect on corporations and organizations when applying it strategically – seems to have failed at being accepted as a "mainstream" approach to innovation. One possible explanation could be that design is often portrayed as a contradiction to the prevailing culture and logics in most boardrooms and R&D departments.

Damien Newman, principal of the California-based design agency Central, once introduced what he called the "squiggle of the design process" – which has become a somewhat iconic, visual representation of what a design process often looks like. On the one hand, it is as genial as it is self-explanatory, but unfortunately, it has also contributed to underpinning the perception that the design process not only differs from, but also comes across as incompatible with, the typically linear and mathematically inspired development processes that most organizations embrace (Figure A).

Provoked by this, as well as other observations, my own experiences, and numerous discussions with business as well as public sector leaders, I have gradually built up an interest in inquiring whether there might be ways in which the organic, cyclic, and iterative design process could be tamed to an extent where it becomes compatible with and easier to integrate into – even enhance – the aforementioned, mainstream linear logic. The outcome of this process of reflection and inquiry is the *INNOLITERACY* model – a wholehearted attempt at creating a common ground for the otherwise seemingly irreconcilable approaches to innovation and development. The model will form a red thread throughout the book, but before introducing it, I want to take you through some of the reflections

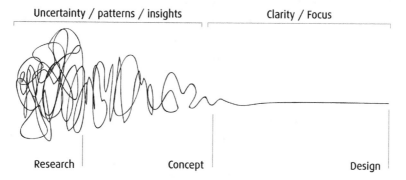

Figure A Damien Newman's "squiggle of the design process"

I have made in the process, and through some fragments – the useful ones – of what has become known as "design thinking" and the rationale behind the claim that design is a key factor in fostering and delivering innovative solutions (Figure B).

The first part of this book deals with the idea and concept of innovation and some of the preconditions, I believe, that need to exist before true innovation can take place. I start out with some reflections on how human beings – disregarding whether their personal and professional profiles indicate that their behaviors are driven by their left or right side of the brain – are encouraged to be part of and contribute to development and change processes; to contribute to innovation – not least in the earliest phases of the development process. I also reflect on how organizations can create a methodological framework and physical conditions, which encourage rather than hamper innovation, and which are inclusive, rather than prohibitive. From the boardroom and senior management down throughout the organization – in any organization – and beyond to clients, customers, or citizens, the intellectual capital is the easiest and least risky to invest in and capitalize on. So much so, that not exploiting its potential and harvesting its dividends is downright mismanagement.

In the second part of the book, I will linger on the concept of reflection and how it enhances our ability to enter into creative and innovative processes, our ability to see new and combine existing possibilities, and our willingness to approach well-known as well as new and unknown challenges in new and sometimes unorthodox ways. The rationale is simple – far too little time is left for ourselves and our colleagues to reflect. Moreover, the physical conditions discourage it and we rarely see it appreciated as related to an organization's innovation capacity. The objective of this part of the book is to argue the importance of time, space, and incentives to reflect – individually as well as collectively, thus stimulating reflection as a systematic and structured approach to accessing intellectual capital such as ideas, knowledge, and experience – resources which can be fed into and add value to the innovation process, but which, far too often, are never given the chance to come into play.

In its third part, I will focus on the concepts of "framing" and "reframing" and argue why it makes a whole lot of sense to reallocate a

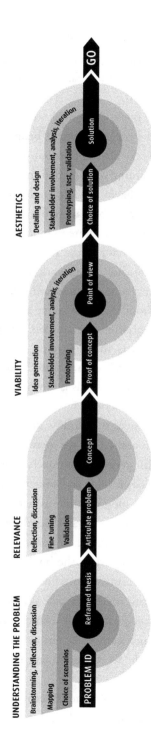

Figure B The INNOLITERACY model

much more substantial part of the resources and investments to the earliest phases of the innovation process than what we see being practiced in most organizations today. The two concepts will be dealt with as integrated elements in a quite familiar context to most professionals – the much used and sometimes misused "stage-gate" model. This linear stage-by-stage approach makes up the framework for a majority of all organizations – regardless of whether they are private or public – and their development activities.

There are countless barriers to embarking on new and less proven methods than a version of an already well-known and uncontroversial, linear, and logical approach such as the one mentioned, and for organizations to "experiment" with something as crucial and sensitive as development and change processes. One such barrier could be that there seems to be a lack of simple models for how to make creative – hence, nonlinear – processes cofunction with more stringent and linear processes, known for all other parts of the organization. My contribution, therefore, includes a model proving that a classical, iterative, cyclic design process can actually coexist and function as an integrated element in a just as classical, linear process as we know it, and where there is certainly no lack of variety and alternatives to choose from. Some of the ideas by which the INNOLITERACY model has been developed are discussed and exemplified in a context of problem solving in general, while some examples revolve around the relevance of applying and rethinking elements known from design practice, such as stakeholder engagement strategies, resource allocation, and how to work with success indicators and assessment in innovation processes.

The fourth part of the book takes you through the INNOLITERACY model iteration by iteration. It is my hope that this part of the book could serve as a guide or a roadmap – even as a checklist – the next time you are engaged in a development project where the outcome has potential consequences for many and where there is something at stake, in particular if the challenge is of such a character that you know which problem to solve, but not necessarily how, by which means, or how to get there.

The fifth and last part of the book deals with how to take, manage, minimize, or downright avoid risks, and how the methodology on which

INNOLITERACY is based and on how concepts and elements such as "user-driven," "user-centered," "co-creation," and "design thinking" – whether they are based on design practice, ethnography, anthropology, or any other human science – all contribute to dealing with the risk of not meeting the needs or demands of the market or the citizens. The objective of this part of the book is to discuss the direct correlation between the choice of methodologies and the likelihood of your process enabling you to hit any given predefined target. Working systematically with framing, reframing, stakeholder engagement, and structured iterations – all parts of what you could call design methodology – could be one of the ways in achieving inner-ten innovation.

PART 1

Innovation, Design Methodology, and the Current Design Discourse

At the heart of the discourse currently influencing design practice, education, and research – as well as political agendas where design has captured a space, however marginal – there seems to be very little space dedicated to the dimension of giving form and shape to tangible artifacts. Most of the space seems to have been occupied by discussions on how design as a methodological approach can enhance the development and innovation of not only products, but also services, business models, and organizations – across industries and in private and public sectors alike. One result has been that the discourse has revolved much more around design thinking than design doing.

If one consults a fairly authoritative source, one of the frontrunners of design thinking, IDEO's Tim Brown, design thinking can be described as a discipline that uses the designer's sensibility and methods to match people's needs with what is technologically feasible and what a viable business strategy can convert into customer value and market opportunity. There might be many more or less parallel and slightly different takes on exactly what the concept encompasses, but in any case, it has, to an almost frightening degree, guided the discussions and approach to what design is and what design can do during the last decade or so. Despite and seemingly totally disregarding that, Harvard University professor of architecture, Peter G. Rowe wrote his book *Design Thinking* in 1986.[1]

---

[1]P.G. Rowe. (1986). *Design Thinking* (Boston, MA: MIT Press).

When the discussion has not revolved around design thinking, terms such as strategic design, service design, and design management will often occur. According to an authoritative source such as Politecnico di Milano's web source, *polidesign.net*, strategic design is a design activity that concerns the product service system, meaning the integrated body of products, services, and communication strategies that either an actor or a network of actors (companies, institutions, nonprofit organizations, etc.) generate and develop to create value. Companies working with strategic design are aware of how products and services influence social ecosystems, people's social lives, their everyday challenges, and how they see themselves, and work systematically and strategically with such insights to add value to their propositions.

The core of service design, on the other hand, is to facilitate, through design thinking, a transaction or exchange between a supplier and the user of a service. It consists of planning and organizing people, infrastructure, communication, and material components of a service in order to improve its quality and the interaction between the service provider and customers. The purpose of service design methodologies is to design according to the needs of customers or participants, so that the service is user-friendly, competitive, and relevant to the customers. As service design has been as – or even more – readily embraced by the public as the private sector, I will often refer to citizens, users, or beneficiaries, rather than customers.

Finally, design management is a specific discipline revolving around managing design processes and facilitating – through systems and organizational interventions – maximum return on the financial, human, and technology resources allocated to a given design challenge or project or to building design awareness and a design-centered culture.

While design professionals and design thinkers have developed their practice and theoretical understanding of design, design is still being kept alive as a lifestyle phenomenon by magazines and newspaper weekend specials, perpetuating the more common understanding of design as a feature differentiating good taste from bad and expensive furniture from inexpensive and as synonymous with fashionable, and interestingly enough, primarily urban living, materialized in fancy cars, garments, and accessories – an approach to design, which has not been *comme il faut* in design circles for decades. Perhaps that also explains why design as a concept points in all kinds of directions, and despite the attention it has been given, has failed – at least so far – to convince the world of its aptness as tool for improvement, innovation, and change.

Despite its adolescence as a concept – steadily growing and maturing, and yet, not yet deserving the respect that grown-ups crave – design has, in fact, proven its potential as a source of inspiration and tool for change, though unfortunately in the most courageous parts of industry primarily. Many of the tools are found in the methodological toolbox of the practicing designer and adapted to fit into the theoretical framework needed to attract attention on a corporate level. The only dimension, which has been from the beginning and still is a pillar in design practice, which rarely seems to reach the pages of management literature dealing with innovation, is aesthetics, a solution's ability to appeal to the emotional and sensorial apparatus of – thus being more likely to be embraced by – the user.

The Starting Point for the INNOLITERACY Model

In the model discussed in detail later on in this book, each one of the iterations I suggest – each stage of the development process or each "round," as I will most often refer to it – has a heading and a fixed and recognizable format throughout to the end. This is primarily to make sure that focus is kept on the objective of the process. It leads us from understanding and validating the problem and its relevance through to the validity and viability of different scenarios and the aesthetical resonance of the final solution. A substantial part of the resources are suggested to be allocated to understanding what the problem is and making sure that we solve the right problem, before even thinking about how to solve anything at all – not to mention what he solution will look and feel like. Then, when the time is right, and we know that we're on the right track, we look at possible ways of making a difference and of developing propositions, which will be sought after and preferred by users, citizens, beneficiaries, or customers. . . .

As such, an obvious starting point for this book would be the famous expression "form follows function" – often used to portray the Danish

Modern era pivoting after the Second World War, but which was actually introduced by the American architect Louis Sullivan in 1896. If the problem is not precisely identified, it makes little sense to solve it, and if the solution proposed is not valid, it makes little sense to go to lengths to give it a form and a shape.

On the other hand, while maintaining that form follows function, it is important not to see this as a devaluation of form itself. It was then – and I believe that it is today – a mere recognition of its logic as one of nature itself, thus not really something to question. When its normative meaning has been discussed over and over again without success, it might be because design is anything but normative. Discussing design requires and deserves a contextual backdrop.

In any case, form follows function in my world, and yet, the aesthetic dimension should never be underestimated, as should aesthetics never be degraded to be a question of visual beauty only. I will discuss aesthetics in more detail in Part 2, but I can already here reveal that to me, aesthetics is all about how an individual or a group of individuals experiences, relates, and connects to a product or a situation. Even though aesthetics – in accordance to mine as well as most other definitions – is of fundamental significance for the user experience, users have rarely any influence on this part of the process, unless they are asked to relate to a final or close to final solution. I will give some examples of how users were or could have been involved. Unfortunately, there are far too many examples of, for example, digital design solutions, where no one ever cared to engage users in the development of a meaningful user interface.

And it is not as if user engagement is something new and untested. One of the most famous personalities from the Bauhaus school in Weimar, and later on Dessau and Berlin, Laszlo Moholy-Nagy, way back in 1923 proclaimed that the whole idea of the "movement" was that "No, this is not about products,...but people." Hungarian-born Moholy-Nagy headed the ground school of Bauhaus from 1923 to 1928, before he decided to work as an independent designer for a decade in Germany and later on in England. In 1937, he moved to the United States, where he established the "School of Design," which later became "Institute of Design," and from 1949, the first in the United States – and still one of the world's leading – academic design educations as part of Illinois Institute of Technology in Chicago.

One of the founders of the Danish Modern movement, Kaare Klint was also convinced that a precondition to design good, properly dimensioned furniture, which would be embraced by its users, was a thorough understanding of the human body, its dimensions and movements, human activity, and sentiments. It sounds so obvious that the need for a book about user involvement in the twenty-first century seems almost superfluous, but unfortunately, that is most certainly not the case, and I cannot stop wondering why that is.

Sometimes, not engaging users in the development process is a conscious choice, and provided the choice is not made out of lack of knowledge of how to engage stakeholders in the process, there is no way I or anyone else can contest it. Most of all because some of the most successful companies I know practice this exclusive discipline quite consistently – from the global coffeemaker maker BODUM to the most common of all examples of an innovative organization; Apple. For the latter, it would probably not be possible to pursue their strategy of building a global hype prior to every product launch if an unknown number of users had had the chance to see, try, and leak the novelties beforehand. For BODUM, it rests in a more pragmatic observation – that after decades of being active in the marketplace for kitchen utensils and household products, in combination with a senior management as well as a fine-masked net of retailers throughout the world with deep understanding of and close dialogue with its customers, their ability to hit the target has proven almost unchallenged, with the involvement neither of users nor external designers. They just know what they're doing and they do it well. Good for them.

On Innovation

So many books have already been written on the significance of innovation, and on how it can be embedded in corporate as well as public sector organizations, that I have quite consciously decided to skip the "what it is and how it works" chapter, which you may have expected as part of this introduction. I have decided to, rather, see my own contribution as support to and a supplement of much of what exists already, without pointing in any specific direction as to where the best source of a basic understanding of innovation is found.

I do, however, have two recommendations for literature, which has helped me understand the field of innovation and the textbook material available on it. One of them is Chip and Dan Heath's book, *Switch – How to Change Things When Change is Hard*,[2] a book, which deals with human behavior at its core and the barriers we all have within us when we are confronted with something new. It not only points toward them, but also describes in a fascinating manner how we can challenge ourselves and prime ourselves to be more receptive to change and the unknown.

The other is a book resembling no other books: *World Changing – A User's guide for the 21st Century*,[3] an anthology with contributions from an impressive range of thinkers within areas as diverse as politics and philosophy, societal and urban development, design and innovation, and with a foreword by former vice president Al Gore, a foreword commencing with these words, "This book is about rising to meet the great challenges of our day." No more, no less.

Moreover, a wide range of web sources offer valuable inspiration and new knowledge on better understanding of and hands-on advice on how to foster change and renewal in companies and organizations – in addition to all the groups available on social media, such as, for example, LinkedIn. Just start searching. But, as this book takes as its departure design management as professional practice and area of research, it seems unavoidable to point to one specific source of insight and inspiration – regardless of whether one chooses to be a member or not – the Design Management Institute (DMI), a U.S.-based organization, which aspires to be international, despite its immediately recognizable roots. Which is OK, in the sense that I would claim as a fact that much of the knowledge we have on innovation, and which will influence European companies and organizations greatly, was developed in the United States.

To me, innovation means to create something new or improve something already existing, by which the perceived or real value of the product, service, process, or transaction is higher than what was previously

---

[2]C. Heath and D. Heath. (2010). *Switch –How to Change Things When Change Is Hard* (Portland, OR: Broadway Books).

[3]A. Steffen. (2006). *Worldchanging: A User's Guide for the 21st Century* (New York, NY: Harry N. Abrams).

possible to deliver. I also need to point out that "perceived or real value" in my world has to do with much more than the bottom-line, regardless of single or triple. It has to do with user experience and the contribution of the solution in question to reach a higher goal, whether that goal can be measured in terms of aesthetics or attraction, accessibility or usability, thought-provoking or taboo breaking. And – just because the whole concept of "value" is so ambiguous, the reflection and intellectual anchoring of any process based on design methodology is so crucial.

Design Methodological Innovation

Innovation taking design methodological empiricism as its point of departure demands a process where not only users, but all possible – however remotely relevant – stakeholder groups are thought into the value chain of which the challenge and the solution is part. Not only on paper, but in practice – systematically and wholeheartedly, with the objective of tapping into all existing and relevant knowledge, sentiments, and biases. It might be cumbersome, and in any case, it requires certain resources, both in terms of manpower and budgets, and it is not in itself a guarantee of a leaner or more efficient process – quite often the opposite. On the other hand, the probability of delivering the most sustainable and relevant proposition available within realistic restrictions is significantly higher. This is not only something that has been tried and experienced by many. It has also been duly and properly documented by research conducted by research institutions and a range of projects funded either by national governments or by supranational bodies such as the European Union. A remaining question, though, seems to be how this knowledge finds its way out and into corporate as well as public sector boardrooms and management teams. Despite the overwhelming number of governmental as well as nongovernmental authorities and agencies in existence, no such mechanism seems to exist – the one dedicated to spreading the gospel of innovation and how its mysteries are solved, its barriers overcome and its tangible results on bottom-lines as well as a handful of other measurable benefits harvested. For the same reason, it seems like there will still be a need – for some time yet – for people like myself and the projects I have been engaged in, to identify and indulge in the flow of new knowledge and new case studies produced every year, supporting the case for design-driven innovation and validating the experiences, insights, and reflections already made. This book is such a reflection in itself – anecdotal in its form, and yet tied up in a model, which didn't seem to exist before – and for which my ambition is to resonate with some of you readers, to an extent where you decide to apply it on your next development project. Start with a smaller one; just a small piece of advice. . . .

For almost two decades, I had the privilege of following the continuously growing interest in concepts related to design and innovation, and in particular, where the two are being seen as parts of the same whole. As CEO of the association of Danish design professionals from 2000 until 2012 – a window in time, where design as a concept has not only changed radically, but also gradually conquered new territories – I have had the chance to follow the discourse closely, whether the discussions had their origins in the professional environment, research community, or as part of political agendas. Many disown design as a key to innovation, while others turn their back on innovation as such, either because of the tendency of such discussions to be rather abstract and downright irritating. As such, design and innovation suffer from the same mix of enthusiasm and rejection as all new concepts, trends, or claims. However, while buzzwords appear, fight for acceptance and space, and then, most often disappear, reality is rather less volatile.

So is the solid, tried, and tested knowledge slowly accumulated as it is put to a test through one of the many aforementioned projects – knowledge of how design-driven innovation improves competitiveness through new and improved, smarter, more effective, and more sustainable products and services. Meaningful innovation in my book is where a new or improved product or service, a new organizational or business model, or changed behavior for the better as a whole contributes to a better experience for users and other stakeholders than any previously existing alternative. Very much in line with Herbert Simon, who said that, "Everyone designs who devises courses of action aimed at changing existing situations into preferred ones."[4]

---

[4]H.A. Simon. (1969). *The Sciences of the Artificial* (Boston, MA: MIT Press).

I have often been surprised at how difficult it has seemed to convince corporate leaders that investing in design and innovation is good business, pure and simple. We do no longer lack documentation or hard-core evidence that using the methodologies, which have always been labeled design practice – provided they are used strategically and systematically – pays off. Methodological approaches such as stakeholder engagement, iterations and cyclic, rather than entirely linear work process, continuous prototyping and focus on the aesthetical resonance of the solution we work toward, all these are vital contributors to the position that many companies and products have in our collective consciousness and in statistics of market penetration and support. And still, we hear again and again that working with design and designers is too risky, as "you never know what you get." Which, by the way, is true – you don't always know at the start what you'll get out of a design process, and that is exactly why it is so valuable. If you knew from the beginning the outcome of a development process, to me, it comes across as almost silly to put so much energy into it. Then, just do it.

What any responsible R&D responsible needs to know, however, is which process, consisting of which elements and documentation of their efficacy and relevance to the challenge in question, he or she believes in and is prepared to endorse. There is no reason why the procurement of professional design and other innovation-related services should be left more to chance than the procurement of any other service, so don't hesitate for a second to be demanding and critical of what you get.

Another argument for not embarking on an unknown journey with unfamiliar elements and less stringency than what is often seen in corporate environments is that one already has well-functioning project management models and tools, with which many creative methods would seem incompatible. INNOLITERACY challenges this assumption – in part, by looking at the assumed barriers for such integration and for putting it to a test, and in part, by proposing an iterative process model, which is clearly inspired by and easy to combine with the majority of the existing and most often distinctively linear models found in modern organizations.

The Significance of Solid, Documented Facts

Denmark was a pioneer with regard to actually documenting design's effectiveness, in 2003, delivering the first quantitative as well as qualitative analysis of the economical effects of design, studying 1,017 companies to identify the correlation between design use and performance. It shows an unquestionable link between using design strategically and the revenue growth, profit, export sales figures, and attractiveness as employer of the companies studied.[5] It also indicates that the companies with the deepest knowledge of design methodologies also benefit the most from procuring design services externally. Other studies, undertaken by players such as the already referred to DMI and the British Design Council, confirm the overall findings.

However, established as an academic discipline and domain, after four decades of struggling to be embraced by the business community, it still surprises me again and again how many executives with R&D, services, or business development responsibilities are utterly unfamiliar with design management as a concept. This is often reflected in corporate communication, where design, innovation, and business development are rarely seen as related. However, it needs to be added that the correlation between the three and the acknowledgement of design management seems far more common in the United States than it does in Europe. North American companies of a certain size often have several design managers among their staff, and design as an approach to the development of new products, services, and business models seems significantly more firmly rooted than what seems to be the case for their European parallels. I found an example of this in a job advertisement from the Akron, Ohio-based tire manufacturer Goodyear – a city, by the way, which both exists as a result of, but which also has suffered from the vulnerability of being totally dependent on the production and sales of tires.

Recently, they sought a *Design Innovation Manager*, and described the job responsibilities with, among others, the following;

This position requires a working knowledge of Primary Research (ethnography, intercept, in person, etc). Demonstrated experience

---

[5]Danish National Agency for Trade. (2003/2008). *The Economic Effects of Design/ Design Creates Value.*

in ideation and portfolio management to drive the commercial-ization of new products, processes and services. Prior work and interaction with third parties as related to designing value proposi-tions. Prior work in designing value propositions around product, service, communications and systems for diverse groups of users. Design analysis and synthesis. Design user-centered value proposi-tions. Behavioral prototyping. Conducting and leading workshops around brainstorming in groups. Secondary research. Project management. Digital, video & physical presentation of findings.

I feel quite certain that numerous European companies hire staff to fulfill some of the same roles – either wrapped in one or dispersed on sev-eral positions – and with the overall objective of securing the company's competitiveness through constant development of new and improvement of existing products and services. However, I do not believe that I ever saw the same degree of articulated connectedness between design and innovation or between "value propositions" and design methodologies, as described in the ad. Perhaps the lack of articulation of what design can do is a primary – or at least contributing – factor in explaining why design is still fighting windmills in many corporate environments.

My own conviction is that corporate as well as public sector organiza-tions, whose managements are well informed about and open to which methods and approaches benefit innovation within their own field – design methodologies included – and whose cultures encourage the individual to contribute to the innovation process, also perform better than the rest.

This book, hence deals with three very different, and yet, closely related components. The first is the ability to reflect and analyze what is needed to encourage individual as well as collective reflection. The other component is the importance of allocating more resources to and of man-aging the very early phases of the innovation process – focusing on fram-ing and reframing and on making sure that one actually solves the right problem. And the third component is the correlation between the two aforementioned and the constant need to minimize risks in the develop-ment process – quite concretely, the risks of developing something which, at the end of the day, is never embraced by the market, by the users, or by the community for which it whom intended.

When wanting to share something, which to one self is important, finding a relevant and perceptive audience is a key challenge. The target group for new knowledge on innovation and creative methodologies is neither clearly defined nor easily reachable. It encompasses specialists and experts, middle management and senior management – in private as well as public organizations, large and small – responsible for delivering and constantly developing new or improve existing propositions, material as well as immaterial, operating in an analogue or a digital environment – or both, business to business, business to consumer, or just human to human. And on top of that, it represents every possible approach and level of maturity when it comes to how things are already done, who one's stakeholders are, and how prepared one's organization is for change.

My claim will be, though, that regardless of which of the descriptions above is seen as appropriate for your own organization, user-centric, iterative, and firmly managed development processes inspired by design practice and methodology will benefit your endeavors at enhancing your organization's innovation capacity and performance. Needless to say, the methodologies need to be adapted and further developed to match the exact objectives, structures, products, or services, and audience, but having said that, there will be lots of inspiration and food for thought to find in the following.

INNOLITERACY

INNOLITERACY is a constructed word, inspired by other and more commonly used words such as eco-literacy and computer literacy – both deriving from the overall semantic family of "literacy" and resonating with a trend, which over the last two decades was referred to as "new literacies," the understanding of and skills within a specific area, introduced by the scholar David Buckingham in his article "Towards new Literacies, Information Technology, English and Media Education."[6] INNOLITERACY, in other words, means the understanding of and the skills to undertake innovation and innovation processes. As a matter of fact, it is rather

---

[6]D. Buckingham. (Summer, 1993). "Towards New Literacies, Information Technology, English and Media Education," *The English and Media Magazine*, pp. 20–25.

closely related to a term, which is already seen quite frequently – design literacy.[7] The difference, as I see it, is that design literacy most often refers to the understanding of the form and shape of an artifact or object, while "innoliteracy" focuses much more on the understanding of the journey leading to how we choose to solve any given problem.

Reflection, framing, and reframing are all stepping stones on this journey, thus prerequisites for meaningful innovation, as well as some of the most fundamental risk management tools we have access to. While we all reflect inadvertently and all the time (in French, to think translates into reflechir – to reflect), we do not always reflect consciously about what we are currently engaged in or the decisions we are about to make. Conscious refection is a targeted activity, giving oneself the opportunity to dwell and linger, instead of just jumping to conclusions.

I have often used children's literature as a starting point to argue the value of a need for an actual and deliberate strategy for all one's undertakings[8]:

"Would you tell me, please, which way I ought to go from here?",
   Alice in Wonderland asked the Cheshire cat.
"That depends a good deal on where you want to get to", said the cat
"I don't much care where –", said Alice
"Then it doesn't matter which way you go", the cat responded.

It does matter where you want to go – not least to choose the right way. Our actions and every single choice we make are all made at the cost of an unknown and often unfathomable number of opt-outs. And just like the goals we choose to pursue determine which process we choose to follow, the results we reach and how close to the articulated goal we get also reflect to which degree the process chosen was the right one. On the same note, if the goal is not precisely defined, we run a great risk of choosing the wrong route, or – as a worst case – of not getting anywhere at all.

---

[7]S. Heller and K. Pomeroy. (1997). *Design Literacy, Understanding Graphic Design* (New York, NY: Allworth Press).
[8]L. Carroll. (1865). *Alice's Adventures in Wonderland* (Charlotte, NC: SBP Editors).

Perhaps we were created that way, but the fact is that many of us often choose the line of least resistance, and often, without having a clear vision of the goal. We seem to be more eager to get moving than to contemplate and make sure that we're heading in the right direction, which means that we sometimes reach out for the most obvious and most comprehensible problem, without being clear about how it contributes to or fits into an overriding strategy or objective.

Sometimes, that's exactly what's needed – for symbolic reasons, to send the right signal or to put out a fire. Sometimes, there is no need to complicate matters or to elevate the process to "rocket science."[9]

But increasingly more often, in organizations relying on a multitude of intertwined and mutually dependent actors and mechanisms – internal as well as external – and where the organization's propositions in the form of numerous product or service propositions are too opaque to understand the complexity at a glance, solving a "random" symptom (the one standing out as obvious to all) can be anything from waste of time to downright devastatingly harmful.

Solving Complex Problems

Complexity breeds complexity. A complex problem calls for a complex solution – not complicated, but a solution as facetted and complex as the problem it's there to solve. In the book *Complex Adaptive Systems,* Scott E. Page and John H. Miller clearly distinguish the difference between the two characteristics:

> We would, however, like to make a distinction between complicated worlds and complex ones. In a complicated world, the various elements that make up the system maintain a degree of independence from each another. Thus, removing one such element does not fundamentally alter the system's behaviour apart from that which directly resulted from the piece that was removed.

---

[9]According to www.phrases.org.uk, the term "*it's not rocket science*" in the 1980s replaced "*it's not brain surgery*", which appeared for the first time in the 1960s, describing something which is not by far as difficult as it's thought to be.

Complexity arises when the dependencies among the elements become important. In such a system, removing one such element destroys system behaviour to an extent that goes well beyond what is embodied by the particular elements that are removed.[10]

Complexity is directly correlated with risk – the more complex a situation is, the likelier it is that crucial factors are disregarded; factors, which may adversely influence the end result. One might just not register the factor at all, or one may mistake the situation for being complicated instead of recognizing its complexity, thus misinterpreting the situation, reaching for the wrong tools to address it and ending up with either a wrong solution, or even more common, the right solution to the wrong problem.

The misunderstanding is widespread. An example can be found on Virgin's website, where the honorable Sir Richard also falls in the trap of mixing the two, as he flags the view that "Complexity is your enemy. Any fool can make something complicated. It is hard to make something simple." Again, complexity is being equaled with complication, and even elevated to being the wisdom of life.

Because there are no simple solutions to complex problems, it also means that entering into solution mode can have quite severe consequences with regard to human as well as financial resources, independently of whether the problem is solved in-house or with the help of eternal resources.

The researcher John Kamensky has captured this quite nicely, by saying that:

Understanding the difference between a complicated problem and a complex one is important for today's leaders. They require different strategies and tools that are largely not interchangeable. Sometimes a problem will morph from one state to the other – either from complicated to complex, or vice versa – so you'll need to be ready to adapt your strategies and tools accordingly.[11]

---

[10]J.H. Miller and S.E. Page. (2007). *Complex Adaptive Systems* (Princeton, NJ: Princeton University Press).

[11]J. Kamensky. (2011). *Managing the Complicated vs. the Complex; Viewpoint Fall/ Winter 2011* (Washington DC: IBM Centre for the Business of Government).

So, to understand the problem and its complexity is of utmost importance to activate the right forces to solve it. It goes without saying that both financially and with regard to deploying other valuable resources, it is quite important that one actually addresses the right problem, and that this has been defined and articulated as precisely as possible. This seems and sounds quite obvious, but isn't necessarily so out there, in the real world. Partly, we all tend to react to symptoms, rather than sourcing the root of evil. We take painkillers instead of taking 3 days off to clear our system of the underlying reasons for the headache. In the same way, we see organizations reacting to low-hanging symptomatic problems instead of relating to their origin. We fire employees with underperformance as pretext, while we fail to analyze whether their competences and conditions for doing the job are right. Or we solve problems with clients' complaints by making the client happy in the situation, by giving an extra rebate or by adding value to the specific transaction, while the underlying reasons for the problem, which may stem from anywhere in the value chain, remains unresolved. Or, we establish yet another web platform or develop yet another app to alleviate an unwanted development – from obesity to stress symptoms, or to underpin a desirable development – from the use of bicycle helmets to more biodynamic consumption. But we far too often do not address the core of the challenges we observe.

To identify the right problem and to assess its degree of complexity is a question about being able to think systemically. Systematically – yes, but systemically, more than anything else. Systemic thinking is all about thinking holistically, contextually, and in terms of value chains.

> Our way forward is what we call "systemic thinking." It is a way of thinking that emphasizes connectedness and enables people to see the bigger picture; one in which owners, solvers, solutions, problem-solving methods and problem descriptions are portrayed as a whole system.[12]

---

[12]J. Boardman and B. Sauser. (2013). *Systemic Thinking: Building Maps for Worlds of Systems* (Hoboken, NJ: Wiley).

Moreover, systemic thinking requires the ability to abstract from and challenge the already existing imagery of the situation at hand. Abstraction is something most of us struggle with – in particular, in professional contexts – as we excel at bringing our expertise and the knowledge that we have to the table as soon as we can, and by doing so, we prohibit ourselves the privilege of dealing with the situation as an opportunity with numerous possible outcomes.

Abstraction requires time and space to reflect, and just as important, it requires an openness to add intuition and tacit knowledge – our own as well as others' – to the formalized knowledge in which our professional identity often rests. Tacit knowledge is silent and unarticulated – thus, we need to give its articulation time for it to become coherent and valuable input to the process.

Of course, it may come across as a paradox to disclose and articulate – to formalize – intuition and tacit knowledge, as it can never be made tacit again. Therefore, it needs to be done only when necessary to avoid drying out the reservoir of tacit knowledge in ourselves and in our organization, as the silence itself is extremely valuable. Somehow, it can almost be compared to an organization's other immaterial assets, such as its goodwill and its intellectual capital. However, managed carefully, it makes sense to source the unconscious and intuitive, as long as we make sure that new experiences and new discourse deposit new tacit knowledge in us, as individuals and as organizations.

Just like our own tacit knowledge is a valuable resource, so is all the people an organization has access to "exploit" – staff at all levels, partners, clients, fans – also part of the organization's intellectual capital and possible sources of innovation or elements thereof.

Krister Ahlström, a well-known Finnish industrialist and chairman of the Finnish Design Roundtable, once said: "The most valuable contribution of designers is that they are able to read the weak signals." By reading the weak signals from all these actors, inspiration for new or improved services, products, experiences – or even business models – can emerge.

We all have good ideas once in a while – some of us more often than others. And in every single new idea hides the seeds to valuable solutions to recognized as well as not yet recognized problems, but for such ideas to grow and mature into sustainable solutions, it takes a set of conditions, which promotes, rather than prohibits such growth.

Left – Right – Forward – Aft

One approach to discussions about how to nurture creativity and innovation is to which extent an organization consists of or is dominated by left-brain or right-brain individuals. When I decided to allocate some space for this discussion, it is because it tends to steer the recruitment of certain types of staff, as well as who is invited to be part of the innovation processes in an organization. Even though the discussion may seem a little old-fashioned and out of tune with the more current attitude that we can all contribute to creative processes, we cannot deny that new ideas and thinking outside of the box comes more naturally to some than to others. But if we really want to approach this physiologically, it takes more than just a distinction between the left and the right side of the brain. There is also the forward and the aft, and the lower and the upper – it all reminds more than anything about a German grammar lection (An, Auf, Hinter . . . and so on).

The theory of the different properties of the two halves of the brain is normally ascribed to the neuropsychologist Roger Wolcott Sperry, who received the Nobel Prize of Medicine in 1981 for his work. His research showed that the left side of the brain – except for "running" the right part of the body – represents logic, focus on detail, words and languages, sense of time, our understanding of mathematics and science, the name of things, analysis and strategies, and our sense of practicality. Actually, a majority of us are left-brainers, and for the same reason, most of us are right-handed.

The right hand side of the brain – adversely – manages the left side of the body, but besides, it is also the "creative" side of the brain, managing our emotions and our ability to visualize and abstract and to think holistically, our beliefs and faith, philosophy and art, fantasies and impulse, our sense of adventure and opportunity. People who are all these things, exposing that they are dominated by their right side of the brain, then ought to be left-handed. That, however, is not the case, and curiously enough, nobody has been able to explain this paradox until date.

So, our left side of the brain supports our linear thinking and in components, while our right side of the brain supports iterative and holistic thinking – what is also known as "gestalt." One side focuses on detail and one on the whole, one produces artists and designers and architects, while the other produces accountants and engineers.

However, that's just half the truth. Others have elaborated on and further developed on the Nobel Prize winner Wolcott Sperry's research. In addition to left versus right – as if it were an electoral campaign – the outer part of the brain, both on the right and the left hand side, the cortex, processes sensory experiences and controls cognitive functions such as thinking, remembering, and making decisions, all being undertaken in four separate areas with each their own functions.

The foremost part of the brain is called the frontal lobe. It deals with conscious thinking, planning, and organizing. It also manages most of our recollection and attention. Moreover, it has fairly significant influence on our emotional life.

Behind it, we find the parietal lobe. It focuses on processing sensory impressions, such as distinguishing between physical pain and more pleasurable forms of impact on our body, such as caresses; it processes information on pressure and temperature; and it also influences on our ability to recognize tactile experiences and control our movements.

Underneath the two aforementioned, we find the temporal lobe, managing sensory experiences such as smelling, tasting, and hearing, besides a major part of our memories. And behind it, just above the cerebellum, we find the occipital lobe, which captures and processes visual impressions.

All these elements, just like the left hand and the right hand side of the brain, are developed to different degrees in different individuals. This means that if we actually want a systemic approach to any given situation, and as many different interventions as possible, it is not enough to balance the number of left-brainers and right-brainers – not even mentioning the tendency of forming a predominantly right-brain team together – we also need to balance the group with regard to the different types of rational and cognitive understanding found in the forward part of the brain with the different types of sensory, visual, and emotional experience found in the aft.

As one can imagine, this really starts to become quite complicated (not complex). My own proposition would be to think along a totally different and much simpler line than balancing quotas of dominance by different areas of cortex. By applying diversity in its simplest form – expressed by individual preferences and styles in clothing and lifestyle, in social and material positioning, cultural affinity and behavior vis-à-vis other people and situations – one secures that all parts of the brain and as many optics on life at large are represented. At the same time as it is useful to know how our brains are constructed, how differently and how significantly that influences on our personalities and preferences, I reject the idea that one part of humanity – based on their cerebral configuration – is better suited to engage in creative processes than the other. Diversity is a quality in itself, and even though an individual is not particularly creative as such, there are many other ways in which one can contribute to development, renewal, and change. Just being reminded that not everyone is a blue copy of oneself contributes to a creative and innovative culture.

One Danish company, which has embraced diversity for real, both as a corporate social responsibility disposition and because they have realized the value it brings to its culture, is Foss, a very profitable, global, and yet, family-owned manufacturer of highly advanced analysis equipment for agricultural and food-processing purposes. By leaving the management of their own staff catering facilities to a vocational school for the mentally impaired, all employees in their kitchen and employee restaurant – except for a few responsible managers – are people with special needs and a different outlook on the world than the rest of the staff. One may argue that well, they are highly profitable, so they can afford the luxury of showing some responsibility. My postulate would be that they are highly profitable because they represent the courage and mental and cultural abundance to weigh diversity over complacency. Actually, a really interesting company and business model is "Specialisterne," which translates from Danish as "The Specialists." It has dedicated itself to enable jobs for people with autism and similar challenges. As a socially innovative organization, it was one of the first companies in the world with a team of specialized IT business consultants, all of whom have a diagnosis on the autism spectrum. More and more companies explore and learn to appreciate the value of true diversity.

PART 2

The Tyranny of Decisiveness

This part of the book will focus on how we create a better starting point for making decisions related to the development of new products, services, and strategies – or for managing a regeneration or change process – by discussing the concept of reflection. The objective of this is to render the idea of working systematically with reflection more relevant, and to discuss how you work with reflection as a professional, in an organizational context and as a methodology.

One of the most prominent and appreciated values of masculinity in our time is decisiveness. Often considered a predominantly male attribute – however increasingly appreciated and adopted by women as well – driven by profitability and risk aversion, determination, and urge of conquest; decisiveness is one of the most sought-after characteristics when hiring managers and others with bottom-line responsibility, in the private as well as in the public sector. Decisiveness has become the very symbol of masculinity and strength, of control and of always knowing what the most appropriate thing to do is – at all times and in any given situation. Unfortunately, decisiveness is often confused with dynamics – or even worse, with effectiveness – and with the ability to avoid any waste of time, always targeted and convinced, always in motion, and always one step ahead. Decisiveness warrants focus on the target, on results, on the bottom-line. It often – however, not always – equals "cut the crap," "get on with it," and "keep moving." Determination and performance focus on delivering and on time.

Indecisiveness, on the other hand, is often regarded as a predominantly feminine privilege – the right to admit the weakness of doubt and bewilderedness, often coupled with a certain degree of submissiveness and lack of courage. I guess it's no coincidence that another word for courage is "balls" – and we're talking neither tennis balls nor volleyballs. While the decisive profile sees the end of discussion and signing the order or winning the argument as the only acceptable outcome, the indecisive looks for the opportunities in keeping the door open, in bringing new alternatives on the table, and in keeping the discussion going for as long as it takes, and in picking it up again another time, as the iterative and organic process is to constantly move a little closer to, yet possibly never actually reaching, the goal. Because nothing is final, everything can be improved, or at least, done in other ways and even, possibly, with better results.

An example many of us will recognize, if having lived with or even worked with someone from the opposite sex or disposition. When moving into a new house or flat, or even office, certain decisions have to be made with regard to how to dispose of the rooms and space available, where to put the cupboard and where to put the flat-screen, so to speak. For the decisive, such a decision is final, except from often also being regarded as quite trivial; done and over with, let's move on to something more important. The indecisive will most probably suggest changes as time goes by – as the space is being lived in or the office being used – based on incrementally sensing and understanding how things work and how they can be improved. Sometimes, these improvements are also made, though often, slowly and gradually to avoid confrontation with the other – the decisive party.

The sharply traced differences between the two genders – albeit undergoing change – are, of course, and fortunately so, distorted. Not least so in boards and managements, we find women who are both more decisive and tougher than many men. Some would even go as far as claiming that it takes both more guts and more "manliness" to reach the top for a woman than what it takes for a man, and then, on the other hand, fortunately again, we see female leaders at the very highest of levels – and even a few men – acknowledging the value of historically female values and attributes.

Nevertheless, whether practiced by men or women, the disproportional focus on decisiveness often leads to both unintended results and a tyrannical culture by sacrificing time for reflection and profoundness on the altar of effectiveness and efficiency. Just like a piece of art, a complex problem will consist of several layers. There are the immediately recognizable, and then, there are the more subtle ones, which are gradually revealed as one keeps studying the object of art, asking questions, discussing, and wondering. For these underlying factors to become overt, often also disclosing the meaning of the piece of art, time and space for reflection is needed. Exactly the same goes for getting to the core of a problem. Unfortunately, though, the trend seems to be faster, instead of better and more carefully measured decisions.

We need a new paradigm. Our time calls for more reflection and more prudence, but also, more courage and more consciousness. Far too many decisions are made – whether the situation craves it or not – hastily on a feeble or faulty basis. Far too often, one out of many possible easy ways out is chosen over one out of few possible, more demanding, but also, more right ones, which also more than implies that the scenario of one right and one wrong decision is a rare one. Obviously, if you are faced with the choice between an orange and a banana, you pick the one of your preference, or if allergic to one, the other one will be an obvious and the only right choice, except from possibly refraining from both. However, that kind of trivial dilemmas must be saved for another time – or rather, leave it up to the individual reader to deal with.

I will also quite deliberately stay away from decisions made under pressure or under abnormal circumstances. Under severe stress, mechanisms such as instinct and intuitively mixed cocktails of previously accumulated experience, knowledge, and attitude are activated.

Our instincts are our remaining beastly mechanisms of defense. Acting instinctively does not observe or require reflection or any other form of intellectual processing of the current situation; one does what needs to be done – full stop. Responding to intuition is something else: a sometimes unconscious, and sometimes, partly conscious deployment of stored experiences and deeply anchored attitudes and ethics, but very little reflection and structured processing is involved.

My interest is primarily focused on the decisions we make, which have or may have far-reaching consequences – often for many people – based on assessment and analysis, either individually or collectively. My concern is, as already brought to the table, that such decisions are often made with haste and – if methodically at all – by stringent, strictly linear and risk aversion-focused mechanisms. This, in particular, comes across as provocative when there would actually be time and rationale for choosing other tools than the Gantt chart and others alike, and in situations where a better result would most certainly be achieved by other means, and by allowing time for reflection and reframing. On the other hand, there is a time for everything, and knowing when to cut through and when to make decisions is a vital element of working more iteratively – as important as knowing who to involve, when, and why in the process itself, and at the end of the day, a question of good management and leadership skills. For the individual participant in the process, it can be difficult to stay on track and red lights are often overlooked. Focus on and professional management of the process, thus, is a fundamental precondition of this new paradigm.

Reflection and Decisiveness

In principle, there is no inherent contradiction between the two, between reflectiveness and decisiveness. And still, they very often appear in juxtaposition as adversaries, as they seem to represent two fundamentally different approaches to life.

Reflection, as a mental exercise, derives from reflection as in a mirrored image. It reflects, not always with great precision, an object or person, depending on the surface by which it is mirrored. This is also the case with a mental reflection, where a situation or idea is reflected by the accumulated sum of experience, attitude, knowledge, and aspirations held by the individual. For the same reason, reflection requires time, as very few of us can access this reservoir of insight immediately and simultaneously. The mirrored image we are confronted with needs to be deciphered and interpreted to make sense. The reason for this is simple. Subconsciously, we have all installed filters and a filing system, which prohibits our accumulated experiences and previous reflections to interfere with and mess up our daily lives. On the other hand, we also know when to reach out for them, and exactly which ones will be relevant and valuable in each and any given situation – still subconsciously and at the spur of a moment.

Decisiveness is a valuable quality, but – as previously described – potentially dangerous if it becomes too dominant and stands in the way of exploiting the potential that reflection represents. Decisiveness is not only about being able to make decisions, but to make them fast and efficiently.

The two last ones very often create the aforementioned conflict – a conflict of fast versus time-consuming, of focus on the goal versus focus on how to get there.

As already indicated, reflection requires the existence of four building blocks – four interdependent components: knowledge, experience, values, and aspirations. The first one is knowledge, regardless of how it has been acquired. The second component is experience, as a mass, as well as individual experiences, but first and foremost, the collated baggage of experience that we carry with us as individuals – our own, unique empirical property, based on our sensual experiences and observations, our successes and failures, all that we have tried "on our own bodies" – as in contrast to knowledge, which is a result of a theoretical and intellectual process. The third component required is a certain set of values, an attitude toward and an outlook on life and fellow beings, on what is important and what is not, an orientation or mind-set.

Finally, reflection loses its purpose, unless the fourth component is also present: a certain degree of aspiration, one's individual or collective desire to reach a goal or to obtain something of a higher value or of greater importance. I will revert to each one of the four components soon.

Knowledge is the most measurable out of the four, and the one which is most often regarded as the most crucial precondition for good decision making. However, we do not always possess more than rather basic and shallow knowledge about areas where we might suddenly need to make a decision. In fact, it is quite likely that our knowledge of numerous domains, where we are expected to make decisions, is rather incremental, as there is a natural limit to how many domains of which each one of us – within reason – can call ourselves knowledgeable and whether we excel at technical, practical, or critical knowledge.[1]

Most people are – except from being averagely informed – knowledgeable within a handful or so, and often interrelated, areas. One might, for example, be knowledgeable about food and wine, design and architecture, aviation and space technology. These can be areas where we have built our knowledge through dedicated training and professional experience,

---

[1]B. Yang, W. Zheng, and C. Viere. (2009). "Holistic Views of Knowledge Management Models," *Advances in Developing Human Resources* 11, no. 3, pp. 273–289.

or through passionate interest and curiosity. Thus, many of the important decisions we are expected to make fall within our professional domain, but still, quite a few decisions fall outside of our professional comfort zone. And yet, we cannot always avoid making decisions within areas where we are admittedly not very knowledgeable.

In some instances, this failure to possess the needed knowledge can be rather easily compensated for by simple sourcing – whether by asking someone or consulting a reliable online or offline source. However, sometimes, we do not even possess the language to understand the knowledge we find or to search for the right information, or we might be too lazy or complacent to even search, and yet, we are still expected to – sometimes even demanded to make a decision. As a matter of fact, we are probably both making decisions, as well as being subjected to decisions made by others, where facts make up only a minor portion of the decision-making material.

Experiences are stored in the brain stem, cerebral cortex, and have to be found and dusted off every time we need them, just like in an old-fashioned filing cabinet or in one's own kitchen drawer – the one with all the different utensils in it, where at least I have to search for a while before I find that specific instrument needed to make a lemon peel julienne every time I use aunt Maggie's recipe for lemon custard, and which happens once a year at the most.

Attitudes and values can be specific or overruling. One has attitudes related to private matters as well as to political and societal matters, and we all have an attitude toward life itself. Very often, we hear ourselves saying, "I haven't really got an attitude towards that," and we are wrong. We might not have articulated an opinion about it – either because it doesn't interest us much or because we were never asked that specific question before, but provided the question allowed for it, we would most probably be able to come up with one, derived from what our attitude is to related questions. In any case, our values and attitudes are constructed from what we have inherited and been raised to believe, the experiences we have made, the knowledge we possess, and the degree to which we are open to being influenced by the people we meet, the context we're part of, and the constant stream of impressions we are exposed to every single day.

Aspirations – just like and closely related to our values and attitudes – are products of our experience and the knowledge we have acquired, but it is also more than that.

An ideal is a conception of perfection or model of excellence around which we can shape our thoughts and actions. An aspiration, by contrast, is an attitudinal position of steadfast commitment to, striving for, or deep desire or longing for, an ideal.[2]

Aspirations contain dreams and visions – elements which are not part of our rational machinery. Most of the time, in our day-to-day decision making, our aspirations play a very submissive part, as there is simply not enough at stake. The very moment our aspirations are drawn upon, we reveal a part of ourselves, which can be both personal and private, so most of us learn to measure it carefully. As social beings, we gradually disclose our attitudes and values through who we are and how we relate to colleagues and other fellow beings, as we share our experiences and argue our points of view as part of the processes we take part in. But our aspirations are more intimate and often stick much deeper than our attitudes and opinions. However, even though most of us keep them to ourselves or share them with great care to only a few, they have a great deal of influence on our professional dispositions and our contribution to processes, where the visions of projects or organizations can be influenced.

Raymond Turner is one of the world's leading authorities on design management and strategic application of design, and among many other major projects, responsible for the design planning and development of London Heathrow Terminal 5 and Heathrow Express, design consultant to a range of international companies, and design in-charge for numerous urban development projects. While I'll come back to Raymond Turner later, for now, he introduced the term "design leadership" and claims that creative leadership is all about having a vision for, and thereafter, to create the future.

Reflection balances the four components – knowledge, experience, attitude or values, and aspirations – and holds them up against the

---

[2]K. Brownlee. (2010). "Moral Aspirations and Ideals," *Utilitas* 22, no. 3, pp. 241–257.

situation at hand and the decision we may or may not be involved in taking; we will focus on those that we will, as well as the complexity of the situation. This takes time, and it calls for a conscious choice of giving reflection a chance.

To some extent, reflection is also about filtrating our most immediate and spontaneous reactions and the most obvious answers to any given question through each one of the four. What do previous and analogue experiences tell me? Do I have the knowledge needed to make a decision or do I need to search for more, and if I have – does the most obvious solution also seem like the smartest one? Will it seem consistent with what I otherwise stand for? And, does it underpin or does it contradict the visions and dreams that make up the fabric of what I believe in?

Later on, I will filtrate some of the decisions we often face and some decisions made by others, but where we might all wish that we had more influence. Through examples, I hope that the qualities that we miss out on by rushing decisions and by not giving ourselves time to reflect become more obvious. I also hope to show that the time needed to linger a little more on the possibilities and choices that we have before irreversible decisions are made is worthwhile. Finally, I will plunge into introducing a more formalized and structured model for the entire reflection process.

Reflection as Shortcut to the Right Decision

While indecisiveness has the color of weakness and submission, lack of courage, interest, or engagement, and is very often attributed to the female gender, decisiveness has the color of control and energy, dynamism, action, and the ability to cut through, and is very often attributed to the male gender.

We are not short on prejudice and biases; they play an unquestionable – however, not always acknowledged – role in which decisions are made with influence on our daily lives, professional and private alike.

Reflection – however more common it is among those who give themselves more time to make the right decision – will often be characterized as gender neutral, especially by the male part of the population. The reason, I guess is, that those who are not necessarily prioritizing time for reflection would still like to see themselves as well reflected, but they would most probably also claim that they do not need as much time to reflect as others, and that they make sure that the reflection does not end up as an intellectual pastime. For many, the activity of reflection is an intellectual and somewhat elevated activity, introverted, and exclusive – something scholars and people with too much time on their hands engage in. Something that would be waste of time for many people, such as mechanics or hairdressers or copying machine sales people, but which, on the other hand, could possibly add to one's image as a little more "reflected" or even smarter than one actually is.

So now, after having insulted a large portion of the grown-up population in the Western world, and without malice, it is a fact that some people see the value in contemplative activities and some do not. On the one hand, a prejudice, implying that one has made a judgment without knowing all the facts or having reflected upon them, and on the other hand, a fact, which has to be acknowledged to exploit the potential of reflection.

I will try to remove reflection from the assumedly elitist sphere and apply it to situations we all run into from time to time, regardless of whether one is an apprentice or literary professor and regardless of whether one's primary decision-making domain is a private or professional one. The only requirements, as already stated repeatedly, are a certain amount of relevant experience, relevant knowledge, familiarity with own attitudes and values, and that one has an aspiration in life, a desire to make the best decision possible. And, of course, that one grants oneself the time it takes.

My claim is – and it is a claim – I cannot substantiate it scientifically, so take it for what it is; my claim is that reflection leads to better quality decisions, where the potentially adverse effects they might have are known in advance, which are assessed among and consciously chosen among alternatives and for which it is easier to argue – as simple as that.

What really fascinates me about reflection is that applying it systematically benefits all parts of one's life; vis-à-vis decisions of the most private character, in relation to individuals, whether close or not and whether the relation is lasting or not, in family matters, social relations, and friendships, in one's professional life and as political beings, formally or informally and whether one's role is that of making or that of influencing others' decisions.

However, as this book is primarily about creating a better environment for better decisions with regard to the development of new or the improvement of existing products, services, and strategies, or to planning, facilitation, and execution of change processes, the following chapters intend to cast some light on the very concept of reflection, while we will get back to discussing it as a methodological ingredient at a later stage.

Prerequisites for Reflection

As already mentioned, there are four fundamental prerequisites for reflection: the existence of knowledge, experience, attitude, and aspirations – all parts of our own personalities. Furthermore, a number of external prerequisites influence our reflections, whereof I have chosen the two most important ones: time and space. All this, of course, will be contested by many and accused of grave simplification, which is OK. One could, of course, discuss reflection from any one among numerous other angles, but focusing on the aforementioned four components is what I believe is the most conducive way of discussing reflection as a means to spur innovation, hence my point of departure.

Prerequisite # 1 Knowledge

The knowledge we accumulate over time – both specialized knowledge of whatever area we are expert in and more general knowledge, either related or complimentary to our own expertise or any other, more or less arbitrary knowledge that we possess – is perhaps the most important catalyst we have for reflection. Our knowledge determines which consequences we anticipate that any given disposition will have. If we know the rules, the theories, the statistics, and relevant specific and factual conditions relating to a situation, our reflection of cause and effect – thus on what to do and what not to do – builds on a solid base. Interestingly enough, though, the role of knowledge as a component of our reflection diminishes over time, as a consequence of growing experience and a more conscious understanding of our own motives, values, and attitudes.

Together with knowledge, one's skills also might play a role in which decisions we make. Knowledge and skills are different and yet closely related, and most of all, skills are composed of knowledge and experience within a specific trade, craft, or topic.

Prerequisite # 2 Experience

Every time any one of us experiences success at our undertakings, and every time we fail, the experience sediments and is stored as en element which will inevitably contribute to shaping all future decisions. Taking time to reflect upon a situation, where the result was not as foreseen means to question the risks as well as the expected outcome of it, what the gain envisaged was – as measured either in time, savings, credits, or credibility – and whether the risk of failure versus chances of success ratio was reasonable and assessed with sufficient care. Or, perhaps risks were run for other reasons altogether. Often, consciously running a risk is motivated by rather irrational and personal reasons – as to prove to oneself that one possesses the guts to challenge destiny or the law, or to show others that one has the courage and the self-esteem to choose what Robert Frost calls "the road not taken."

Two roads diverged in a yellow wood, And sorry I could not travel both
And be one traveler, long I stood, And looked down one as far as I could
To where it bent in the undergrowth;
Then took the other, as just as fair, And having perhaps the better claim,
Because it was grassy and wanted wear; Though as for that the passing there Had worn them really about the same,
And both that morning equally lay, In leaves no step had trodden black.
Oh, I kept the first for another day! Yet knowing how way leads on to way,
I doubted if I should ever come back.
I shall be telling this with a sigh, Somewhere ages and ages hence:
Two roads diverged in a wood, and I – I took the one less traveled by,

And that has made all the difference.

R. Frost. (1916). *Mountain Interval* (New York, NY: Henry Holt and Company)

Whichever experiences we have as we move along will influence our actions and reactions forever after, more or less consciously and more or less reflected. Most often, we store our experiences without reflecting upon them as they occur, but they may very well be activated at a later stage, when we face a situation either resembling the first or where a given experience may come in handy and relevant – either consciously, subconsciously, or unconsciously – thus contributing to a more qualified and better choice this time around.

Prerequisite # 3 Attitudes

One's fundamental values and views on life itself, the pillars on which one's life is built, will also influence on how much, how, and in which situations we indulge in reflection. The latter, in particular, as we generally reflect very little upon issues on which we have no influence or which are deeply and firmly rooted in our own private norms, whether defined by religious conviction or by other social and cultural mechanisms.

Attitudes can be individual, but also collective, in the form and shape of a generally accepted norm or culture, a determining factor for what we consider as normal and socially acceptable. However, as this book primarily focuses on decisions made within an organizational context, and where the right to serve and to make decisions depends on a certain ability to observe organizational norms, I will concentrate on which influence others' norms have on our own individual choices and reflections.

Regardless of how individually focused we are, the society and culture to which we belong or subscribe do have a rather significant influence on whether and how we reflect upon any given event. In a society, culture, or organization where the opinions and judgment of others mean a lot, failure will often be perceived as more severe, even shameful or embarrassing, influencing on the degree of courageousness displayed and risks one is willing to run – unless one belongs to a group of individuals, where choosing the road not taken is valued and appreciated, thus benefitting one's identity and peer recognition. In any case, though, no man is an island, and we will inevitably be influenced by the reactions of others, whether articulated or silent, and influence our reflections and choices made the next time we face a similar situation.

Our attitudes do have a significant influence on our reflections, our decisions, and how we relate to the world around us, and they also determine to which extent the importance of others' recognition outplays one's own aspirations and ideals.

Prerequisite # 4 Aspiration

The fourth prerequisite for reflection is the presence of an aspiration – something one is willing to fight for, and which awakens a passion within. One's ideal scenarios and the dreams one pursues influences the desire as well as the ability to learn from one's experiences, regardless of whether the ideal is to become more courageous, more decisive, more generous, or more firm, or whether one's passion is to fight malaria or to fight for world peace. What matters is that one possesses a desire to move on from the current toward something better; otherwise, reflection is meaningless and a waste of time.

To the four prerequisites already listed, numerous other factors may or may not influence one's talent for and one's benefit from reflection. Clearly, one's intellectual capacity plays a vital role, as does one's cultural sensitivity and one's literacy of both one's own and other languages and the ability to articulate thoughts and ideas. In a professional context, six different kinds of competencies are often mentioned: organizational competencies, core competencies, technical competencies, behavioral competencies, functional competencies, and management competencies. The degree of formal and informal competences as well as one's influence on other people and their expectations of the individual in question – all of this influences to which degree one feels obliged to do the right thing and to make the best possible choice, not only because it's important to oneself, but also because it's important to others.

Legislation, rules, and regulations as well as custom, habits, and tradition – what is and what is not *comme-il-faut*, what one can and cannot get away with, and which sanctions can be foreseen if any of these directions are disregarded – also influence one's reflection and to which degree one's decisions are based on one's own rather than others' set of values.

All these factors – and more – and the role each one of them plays in any individual's outlook and points of view have a great deal to do with the individual's own profile and character, but they also influence quite generously the quality of our decisions and our ability to work constructively with reflection as a tool for personal and professional development.

In addition to the already mentioned "internal" prerequisites, two more "external" factors – facilities, if you will – also play a vital role in successfully applying reflection as a tool.

Prerequisite # 5 Time

There's no way around it – reflection takes time – however, it is not necessarily time stolen from something else. The kind of reflection which is not schematically and methodically applied can, instead of "unconsciously" enjoying or disliking a situation – whether already passed or coming up – by using the same time and energy more "constructively" and by trying to actually relating to and reflect upon the situation, be quite valuable. Both retrospective and advance reflection are equally important components of building a solid base of experience, even though they serve two different purposes at the time that they are applied.

For the structured and more methodical reflection – the one that we often skip because we see it as an extra and time-consuming "step" toward any given goal – it is true that it needs to be "scheduled" and prioritized, possibly also at the cost of something else. But for the most of us, both at work and at home, time is quite abundant. I simply do not believe people who constantly claim that they have no time on their hands and that they are constantly busy doing something important and something that contributes to any kind of value creation.

On the other hand, the return on the time invested in reflecting upon a situation or question of importance is, on average, higher than any other investment I can think of, including stocks and bonds, bricks, or vintage wine or whatever else your investment profile dictates. And why should we be less meticulous about how we manage our intellectual capital than we are at managing our finances and other assets? It requires, of course, that one has the ability to distance oneself from the traditional image of dividend – something we expect regularly and in measures that can be counted and recorded (and paid taxes from). The dividend of reflection is rather intangible, as it comes in the form of a higher probability that your choices and decisions are the best possible ones. The upside is that it is not vulnerable to ups and downs in the market, to financial crises, or unpredictable rating agencies, and it can be reinvested immediately and at no extra cost. Actually, I also believe that it can deliver tangible and measurable results over time, but it is hardly measurable before a sufficient number of projects and undertakings have been carried out, and where structured reflection has been built into the process.

Is it possible to identify the direct correlation between the amounts of time invested in reflection and the quality of the decision made? Probably not, but I do believe that if you know that your decision has been made with care and after careful and systematic consideration of cause and effects, you will feel much more reassured and be able to defend your decision much more firmly and with greater conviction. And, that in itself is a quite tangible return on investment.

We make informed decisions every day. Do I take the bike, public transport, the car, a taxi . . .? Do I follow her home, or would it be better not to . . .? Do I stay in for lunch or do I skip and do the groceries . . .? Do I offer myself voluntarily to coach my new colleague and make sure he or she anchors well, or do I stick to what's my formal responsibility . . .? I could go on and on, but from here on, I'll stick to the professional arena and leave the domestic decisions until another time.

Adding to all the above, just as important it is not to be bullied by the expectation of everything to be fast and efficient, it's also important not to be bullied by a self-imposed expectation that every single decision one makes is thoroughly reflected and negotiated at length. We all need to be impulsive and cut the crap in between, and we all benefit from making mistakes and learning from them. Otherwise, life would be unbearable and boring – and innovation would be rare, by the way. As Steve Jobs is attributed to saying, "Sometimes when you innovate, you make mistakes. It is best to admit them quickly, and get on with improving your other innovations."

So, one has to be prepared for reflection taking time and to see it as an investment, and for that reason alone, it has to be managed as carefully as any other available resource.

While we can decide on turning the reflection knob up and down as we wish in our private lives, in our professional lives, seeing reflection as a methodical development tool, we need to be prudent and conscious about how much time we devote to it and prior to which decisions or actions. I will get back to how to deal with this later in the book.

Prerequisite # 6 Space

Umair Haque, who is director of the company Havas Media Labs, author of several books, and listed among the world's most influential thinkers of management and innovation, "Thinkers50," in a *Harvard Business Review* article called for a better doing/reflecting ratio:

> We seem to be clueless about making room for deep questioning and thinking: reflecting. Our doing/reflecting ratio is wildly out of whack. Most action items might just be distraction items – from the harder work of sowing and reaping breakthroughs that matter.[3]

Better conditions for pursuing intellectual processing of the questions and situations we face on a daily basis are not something that should be left to the individual and his or her personal priorities. Actually, the individual should not be expected to decide on how much and when to take time for reflection at work, and as individuals, none of us can decide on making it a natural, respected, and recognized professional activity. It has to be addressed as a structural and political element of the framework offered to individuals, something which is encouraged and facilitated by organizational policies and culture. Part of being a modern human being is our dependency on others' assessments, decisions, and choices, leaving many of us primarily with choices of marginal significance and decisions, which are expected to be made "quick and dirty." Hence, the

---

[3]U. Haque. (November 24, 2010). "Making Room for Reflection is a Strategic Imperative," *Harvard Business Review*.

responsibility of providing time and room for reflection rests with those who are also responsible for corporate culture, strategic direction, and for which goals to pursue.

All the way from primary school – hence, before the prerequisites for reflection are all fully developed – and all the way through to old age, we face "structural barriers" for reflection. One structural barrier is time; the time not granted – we want everything to be fast and efficient – as well as the time we live in failing to appreciate and acknowledge reflection and profoundness as value-creating activities. Not being sure is seen as a weakness, not strength; answers are rated higher than questions; and metrics rule. One might go as far as claiming that we have become less and less intellectual over time – less able to relate to the abstract and the unknown, and to rationally and objectively reflect upon the world around us, at least to the same extent as we excel at new technologies and economic growth.

One might question whether this is a result from conscious choices made by whoever defines the rules, or whether the decreasing level of intellectuality is a result of decreased intellectuality, so to speak. Have we capitulated at valuing this component of classic formation, defined as "relating to the ability to think in an intelligent way and to understand things, especially difficult or complicated ideas and subjects"[4] because we are no longer able to recognize the value it adds?

One of the fundamental assumptions for this book and its justification is my own belief that the people, the decision makers, possessing the power and influence it takes to facilitate reflection by providing both time and space to do so have not altogether lost their own ability to reflect and dwell. I somehow choose to make the assumption that deep within politicians and bureaucrats and corporate leaders, there is a certain degree of confidence in the potential of reflection and a will to recognize its value – provided the arguments for doing so are strong enough, and the value created through reflection matches the time devoted to it.

Going back to room for reflection, to a certain extent, room and space need to be understood as mental room and space, and an understanding of the nature of reflection. But it should also be understood quite literally, as in creating physical rooms and spaces, which encourage reflection and

---

[4]Macmillan Dictionary.

contemplation. All the way through school, I was dreaming of "silent carts" just like in the trains where instead of constantly working in groups in high-ceilinged, frigid rooms painted in an unidentifiable yellowish color, one could retract and indulge in one's own thoughts. That never happened.

As a parallel, I would have wished that the organizations I have worked for since had provided space for oneness and for meetings between individuals – room for contemplation or conversation – what some architects call unprogrammed space, where no one expects you to perform or produce anything in particular, but where staring into the air or reading a magazine or thinking out loud would be welcome, but which were equally suitable for conscious, structured, and targeted reflection. "People need both overview and intimacy. This requires 'unprogrammed' spaces, resembling delta landscapes – overview, plains, caves and crannies."[5]

The challenge exists partly in being able to detach oneself from technological remedies such as mobile phones and tablets, but also in convincing oneself that the introverted activity that reflection is gets promoted from being considered asocial, thus somewhat suspect and counterproductive behavior to being embraced as an activity for which consideration and respectfulness is shown. If our current perception of overt reflection were liberated from its suspicion of useless idleness, it would be much more natural to upgrade it as an activity in its own right, thus also an activity with its own right to suitable premises to be pursued, just like we establish spaces for physical activity – playgrounds to play in and football fields to play football, or other dedicated spaces such as canteens to eat one's lunch. We're just not there yet, possibly as a question of priorities, or rather more likely because we've had our backs turned toward all that is not obviously and measurably productive activity, failing to see the potential value of contemplative and introverted behavior.

At home, we decide – at least to some extent – how we want to dispose of the square meters available, and yet, we make decisions which discourage rather than encourage solitude, as we prioritize big, multifunctional rooms designed to facilitate everything from cooking and hospitality to school homework, home entertainment, and power napping – at once.

---

[5] D. Mandrup. (February, 2003). From the conference "*The Aesthetic Organisation,*" Copenhagen Business School.

Perhaps our domestic lives would also benefit from granting the individual a little more space for and ownership of own thoughts – at least just once in a while.

Back to the office, which I keep reminding myself that this book is all about, where decisions are made on behalf of the department or company, the public body or institution, and all those whose futures will be affected by them. In all these places where new wisdom or new products or new services are developed, nowhere will you see or find much room for reflection. At least, that's the general rule. Only very few companies or organizations have dedicated space – physically and mentally – to step back from the bustle and reflect as an individual or as a group of individuals, if that is deemed to serve the purpose better.

In other words, both time and space – in the widest sense of the word – need to be given if one believes in the value of reflection beyond the few stolen moments during a hectic workday, either in the elevator or the unmentionable, on our way home (where it's often too late), or standing in line to be served at the supermarket cash register, despite the often noisy or visually disturbing environments characterizing such places. I will spend some time later on in this book to discuss how suitable spaces for reflection are actually made for reflection to happen as a strategic, structured, and methodical approach to innovation and change.

One could extend the reflection to how one makes sure that people who are not a permanent part of the organization, but whom we have already identified as important and valuable contributors to innovation processes – people such as clients and suppliers and partners and other stakeholders – are also offered inspiring and inclusive facilities to join in and partake in the reflection process, together with and on equal terms with internal staff. But for all this to happen, reflection has to be built in to the culture and DNA, and into the structured processes of the organization.

Reflection Does Not Equal Free Play

Just to make sure that all are on the same page with regard to what it is that reflection as an integrated part of structured processes means, it makes a whole lot of sense to steer people's reflective activities to a certain degree. One might, for example, ask people to reflect upon any given challenge or problem in light of where it sits in a chain of transactions or in a hierarchy of understanding.

An old example that most of us have run across at some point is Maslow's pyramid, classifying and prioritizing our needs – from physical needs via our need for safety, social belonging, personal or egotistical needs, to our need for self-realization as the highest. The pyramid reflects the importance of the specific needs – physical needs being most important and self-realization least, and the view that a need can only be addressed when the underlying need in the pyramid has been fundamentally fulfilled. Glenn Jacobsen[6], a Danish consultant and author, in 1999 turned Maslow's pyramid upside down. His thesis was that physical needs and the need for safety are not any longer important to people, as they take them for granted, and that for a modern human being, everything starts with self-realization.

No matter which one is right – or least wrong – the framework of their thinking is relevant. Which needs does our organization fulfill – and for whom? If we are suppliers of corporate lunch schemes, what is it that we deliver? Is our mission to make sure that people do not starve? Do we deliver reassurance that the individual gets a healthy and nourishing meal every day, and that the quality and level of hygiene is acceptable? Or, do we deliver a context for human relations between colleagues? Or, do we provide a space for the individual to express him- or herself through their choices of what they take from the buffet? The answer is quite determining for how to develop and improve and innovate the service provided, and having a common understanding of how we see ourselves is crucial for the individual member of our team to understand how he or she is expected to or invited to contribute. Prior to a "product development session," I would have given all members of the team, internal as well as external, the assignment to reflect and elaborate upon what it is that we do offer today, and whether we could possibly offer something else or something more.

---

[6]G. Jacobsen. (1999). *Branding in A New Perspective – More and Other Than Branded Goods* (Copenhagen, Denmark: CBS Press).

A "reflection brief" can take many angles, shapes, and formats. If the process in question is an "organic" and ongoing evolution, rather than a targeted product or service development process pointing toward a specific date of launch, one could, for example, encourage people to reflect upon which barriers they see from their own cubicle or desk to this "new stuff" being welcomed and embraced by the organization at large, or to reflect upon some predefined, statistically quite significant barriers for organizational development.

The Dutch researchers Henk Kleijn and Fred Rorink[7] have identified the seven most common and most significant psychological motives to resist change. They are: fear (I don't know if I can handle it), guilt (I could never subject my colleagues to this), alienation (will the change make me superfluous), infringement (do I retain my privileges), own needs (will the change hamper my career), threat (this will weaken my position), and uncertainty (I have no idea what this will mean to me). Before embarking on such a process, or as a stage along the way, it would be quite valuable for each member of the team to reflect on whether they possess any of these worries or inhibitions – thus, motives for not really embracing the process and contribute fully to it – but also, to ask people to reflect upon how these fears can be met, reckoning that somewhere in the organization, they will exist and possibly be a peril to the process itself.

Reflection as a Contextual Framework

Reflection – or to act or relate consciously reflective toward – can be observed as a contrast to its two opposites, to act or relate either "instinctively" or "intuitively" as previously described. They both seem to prevail across managements and boardrooms all over the world, some more based on stored experience and insights than others, being directed by inherited mechanisms of defense.

I cannot help thinking about how many situations would have been handled differently, how many decisions would have been of a higher

---

[7]H. Kleijn and F. Rorink. (2005). *Verandermanagement: een plan van aanpak voor integrale organisatieverandering en innovatie* (*Change Management – A Plan of Approach for Integrated Organisational Change and Innovation*) (London, UK: Pearson Education).

quality, and how many relations between management and staff and between managers would have thrived if the individuals in the position of making decisions – often with wide-ranging consequences – had dared to give it some extra time, to process the situation intellectually through reflection, and consulted other points of view than one's own, instead of acting on impulse, whether instinctively or – at best – intuitively on the spot.

The obligation; that's what I see it as – the obligation to reflect – has to be seen alongside the power and influence, and not least, the responsibilities embedded in one's position. The more influence and power, and the more responsibility, the greater one's obligation. Responsibility is a rational and measurable entity, often linked, and at least related to compliance. Obligation is more diffuse, less tangible and less measurable, and rather, related to conscience than to compliance. Obligation is a moral rather than legal issue and comes from taking on – instead of or as a result of having been given – a responsibility. Power can be executed in reflected as well as nonreflected ways, and living up to a formal or legal responsibility one has been given can be done without any trace of passion, while taking responsibility (to feel committed and obliged) requires reflection on the power vested in one's position.

Reflection for reflection's own sake is a luxury and something that we should never undervalue or underestimate. But as a strategic tool, reflection is only valuable if contextualized, just like design – which is quite uninteresting in itself, and only becomes meaningful and valuable as phenomenon and methodology when it becomes part of a context including a sender and a receiver, an idea, a material (tangible or intangible), a production line or a transaction, financial, technological, and ethical as well as aesthetical considerations. All these elements create a context needed to manage and inspire the process forward toward a predefined goal. When referring to design, it is clearly because I see reflection and the creative parallels of the design process as closely related and inseparable, and because the whole objective of discussing reflection in this book is to argue its relevance alongside design thinking and design practice as an integrated part of any innovation process, as a management tool, and a means to manage and reduce risks. As such, it also serves as a bridge to the core of INNOLITERACY – scoping, framing, and reframing, and reflection as preparation and prerequisite for, as well as ground pillar of, the creative process.

Reflection as a Management Tool and Source of Innovation

In her first bestselling book,[8] Susan Cain salutes the introverted part of the population and their ability to make decisions powered by the fact that they spend much more time reflecting upon the impressions they receive than extroverted individuals. At the same time, she points toward another fact; that in our Western culture, we both misunderstand and underestimate the contributions of the introverted and the resource they constitute.

In a time, where being able to position oneself is key to success, taking time for reflection can be a brake to one's career, but it does not change the fact that the quality of decisions made after a certain degree of reflection in general is higher than those notoriously shot from the hip.

Professor Joseph A. Raelin has dedicated part of his research to what he calls "reflective practice." One of his own reflections is whether our current times allow for reflection:

> Reflective practice is possible or practical in this age of the busy corporate executive who is socialized to be the person of action, not of reflection. In our turbulent global environment, it appears almost definitional that we need managers, who can inspire reflection to the extent of generating new ways of coping with change. A reflective culture makes it possible for people to constantly challenge without fear of retaliation. Yet, a culture that permits questioning of assumptions is difficult to tolerate because it requires that people in control lose their grip on the status quo.[9]

---

[8]S. Cain. (2012). *QUIET: The Power of Introverts in a World That Can't Stop Talking* (New York, NY: Crown Publishing Group/Random House, Inc.).

[9]J.A. Raelin. (2002). "Don't Have Time to Think! versus The Art of Reflective Practice." *Reflections* 4, no. 1. Society for Organizational Learning/MIT, Boston.

Another senior within management and organizational theory, Edgar H. Schein supports that point of view. He goes as far as to lament the fact that almost no one smokes any longer – though not from a health perspective, but from an organizational theory point of view;

> Many people will not stop for a relaxing tea and pastry (and a bit of reflection) because they may be seen as "wasting time" sitting at a café. Let's begin by reflecting on why we don't reflect more. Most of us don't smoke anymore, but maybe the "smoke break" should be brought back as an institution to provide 5 to 10 minutes of reflection time out on the balcony. Instead of bringing our coffee back to the desk, what about taking a coffee break to walk around the block or to sit alone staring at the landscape and reflecting? [10]

A culture allowing for reflection time and encouraging reflection by allocating suitable spaces to do so needs to come from the very top of an organization. If the CEO has a frenetic personality and behavior, the likelihood that the rest of the management team dares to encourage a more laidback style and coffee breaks on the balcony is rather slim. If time and space are given to enjoy and cherish the small spaces of slack time that most of us experience during a day at the office, and to embrace and exploit them, it is more than likely that the individual member of the team will give birth to more and more and valuable ideas than if the culture demands that we all look terribly busy all the time.

I will revert to some more reflections on corporate and organizational culture in a while.

So, on the one hand, good management allows for time and space for reflection by sending signals and ideally also by practicing that slack time and taking time for reflection are valued. On the other hand, a more structured and targeted strategy to encourage individuals to reflect upon their own roles in the organization, the organization's overall activities and performance, current issues of concern or the coming of spring – you get the idea – can be even more valuable, either on its own or in combination

---

[10]E.H. Schein. (2009). *The Corporate Culture Survival Guide* (Hoboken, NJ: Joseph Wiley & Sons).

with the first. As a management tool, reflection can turn slack time into productive time, no matter how paradoxical it may sound, praising slack time to the skies just a minute ago. One can actually allocate and dedicate time for the individual team member to step back from his or her role and space for a certain amount of time a week or month, paired with a certain degree of engagement in how the time is being disposed. Let's say that every member of staff is given one day a month to reflect – either literally a day or the equivalent time spread out over a month – left up to the individual to decide. What's important is that he or she is committed to do something that could encourage reflection and new ideas. One part of the deal could be that the time is not spent on activities which normally fill up the individual's free time. Reflection time is not free time – it is work. And since it is work, the management should be free to hand out "assignments" – areas of concern, where they would appreciate the team member's input. I heard about companies sending their R&D staff to fairs and trade shows, which are as remote from and unrelated as possible to their own industry – just to look for possible inspiration and solutions which could possible "travel" across to their own industry and inspire innovation. The contract is simple: report back with and share your own personal experience from the show; then, we'll take it from there. No other commitments and no pressure on return on investment.

However, structured and systematic reflection does not require that you dedicate half or whole days to do so. Where it becomes really interesting as a management tool is where it's built into managed processes of innovation, business and organizational development – aiming at accessing the tacit knowledge and accumulated experience of individual team members, and which would never come to the surface, unless written into the process itself. Such processes otherwise often reflect the pace and prevailing culture of "he, who shouts louder. . . ." To benefit from the contribution to such a reflective process, it is crucial that all team members are assured that their input is valuable, and that everyone is expected to listen to his or her own guts to decide on when, how, and to which extent to play an active, and ditto more subdued, role.

This structured and managed approach to reflection, however, is more effective if the aforementioned facilities are in place, so that looking inwardly – as individuals and as a team – feels natural and is experienced as part of how we do things around here. Hence, it becomes part of the planning phase of any project to build in time for reflection as a catalyst of better ideas and a more facetted dialogue with project stakeholders, thus bringing in valuable input that would otherwise have been lost.

Reflection and the Risks That We Run

The correlation between allocating sufficient resources to – and doing the right things in – the early phases of a development process and the risks of failure at hitting the nail at the end of the process is the core of the third part of this book. Hence, at this stage, I will merely introduce you to the idea. For decades, the design industry has had to face the claim that using design and working with designers involves varying and immeasurable degrees of risk taking. "One never knows what comes out of it" has been an argument, leaning up against the lack of metrics to measure the direct effects of design methods and design practice. And by the way, "we don't really understand what it is that you do." The design industry and its advocates have all accepted the claim, and met it with the counter argument that all creative processes involve a certain amount of risks, and that one has to believe that it actually adds value at the end of the day.

Not until around a decade ago, one was really taken seriously when claiming the effects of design, and for one good reason. Before that, very little research existed to document what design can do to products, services, and organizations, but from then on, it has been more and more acceptable to argue the role of design – and of design management as possibly one of the most effective measures to manage and actually minimize risks in development processes. Applying design methodology onto a process means that the challenge at hand is more carefully scoped and framed, that more options are searched and found, that more stakeholders are involved, that the process becomes more transparent and that the process leads to more viable scenarios and alternative solutions than any other process. It also means that possible solutions are prototyped and iterated throughout the process, facilitating qualified choices and decisions before the investments are so heavy that failure is fatal.

So far, so good, but what does reflection have to do with minimizing risks? Well, for me, it's quite obvious that the more questions are asked and the more people with their individual backgrounds and angles are involved in the very early dialogue around which problem to solve and what to do about it, the more likely it is that the right challenge, the right project, is being defined. And what is the right challenge, then? The only thing I know from experience and from having monitored a number of projects is that it's not necessarily the one that first comes to mind. Very often, we solve the problem we see – the most conspicuous one – and alas, quite often only a symptom of other problems, or even a pseudo-problem, thus wasting valuable resources without ever getting to the core of the problem. If that's the case, it quite naturally influences the ROI, and often means that the only option is to start over again. In the meantime, one's competitors might have solved the right problem or addressed the right need, or the citizens have moved to a neighboring community, or the costs of symptom treatment are crashing all conceivable budgetary constraints.

Allocating time for reflection at the early stages of exploration – where the core of the problem is gradually identified and an understanding of its complexity emerges – also means that the right stakeholders and critical factors are built into the process from as early on as possible. By doing so, the project is anchored from day one and the risk of rejection is minimized, instead of being victim to the "not invented here" syndrome – a powerful mechanism that is often activated toward projects and results, no matter how good they might be – which are perceived as being pushed down the throats of the users.

A reflective approach to any problem or situation one faces – often, more a complex of problems rather than an isolated one (they are rare and far between) – and relevant engagement of users and other stakeholders throughout the process contributes to allocating the resources smartly and to reducing risks of pitfalls and hostile interventions along the way, or simply that the end result is being dismissed.

Structured and managed creative processes are not necessarily collaborative or reflective. Some creative processes are perceived as truly intuitive and often unstructured beyond belief. And where that's the case, it is fine and probably the only way, as long as the end result is a new work of art – whether in words, or music or on canvas or in clay, and even sometimes, when the expected outcome is a new product, or space or frock or scenography. However, if the desired outcome of a creative process is a new process or experience, relation, interaction, or transaction or a product or service, for that matter, which requires decoding and broad acceptance in a marketplace or community made up by numerous individuals with their own preferences and biases, collaborative, structured, and well-managed creative processes are much more likely to lead to success. And in those processes, reflection is one out of several means of achieving precision and accuracy when scoping and framing the challenge as well as the possible paths toward its response.

Corporate and Organizational Culture – Management and Chaos

Culture has become just another "rubber word" that can be used to describe a range of different things, depending on the context and purpose of it. From the outset, it encompasses the values and the material as well as immaterial production that we leave to our successors, to the next generation. Applied to a company or organization, it expresses the behavior, mind-sets, and values as well as the goals that its leadership encourage the entire organization to pursue. Some companies are well-known for strong and firmly vested corporate cultures – for example the Danish, yet global company Maersk – for many, mostly known for their star-adorned containers; or Google, for that matter, while other companies and organizations are less conscious of and concerned about their culture. This would typically mean that the culture is more fragile and plays a less prominent role in the lives of its people. It does not mean, however, that it has no culture – all organizations do, and it is the corporate management at any time, who is responsible for which culture characterizes the organization. Is the management accessible, open, and inclusive, and does it encourage dialogue and collaboration, or does it focus on the individual performance and on competitive behavior between staff members? Does it value diversity or does it nurture a certain type of staff members and a certain professional profile? Does it encourage and acknowledge or does it reign by criticism and mistrust? At the end of the day, it all depends on the management principles, values, and mind-sets, which principles, models and means an organization utilizes to reach the goals they have defined.

It seems to be more or less commonly accepted that innovation – at least in the sense and meaning of the word that I lean up against: development, renewal, and change rooted in a constant search for improvements through better understanding of and engagement with relevant stakeholders – can only take place in an environment of openness, inclusiveness, and diversity, managed by principles, such as recognition and trust. For the same reason, many organizations now strive to excel at the same. As innovation was slowly capturing the headlines and the attention of mainstream companies, the Danish professor Anders Drejer said in an interview that corporate culture and work environments might be the single most significant barrier for innovation;

> Far too many corporate managements try to implement new business concepts by help of the existing organisation and by moving boxes and arrows around on their organisational charts – far too often to consider the need for behavioural change for innovation to succeed. Could that possibly also explain why so many innovation projects fail?[11]

Some years ago, a colleague of mine introduced me to the idea that to encourage innovation, you actually need to allow for – even create – a certain degree of chaos. Looking further into this idea, I came across the book *The Chaos Imperative: How Chance and Disruption Increase Innovation, Effectiveness, and Success*. In an interview with *Forbes* magazine, one of the authors, Ori Brafman says:

> "In times of uncertainty, the temptation is to create more structure and order. Because that feels safe and predictable. However, in times of uncertainty you also need a lot of innovation and often times the way to foster innovation is by bringing organized chaos into the system" and continues "Chaos is scary because it is uncontrollable and unpredictable but companies can actually contain chaos and seed pockets of it throughout their organization.

---

[11]A. Drejer. (February 2008). "*There is a major communication challenge – or several – in innovation*" MOK Magazine # 29.

The idea here is that chaos can be extremely productive force, the question though is how to manage it."[12]

Ever since I encountered this appraisal of chaos as a driver of innovation, I have reverted to the ideas that it represents. We need better understanding of the correlation between organizational structure and values on the one hand and the desired development on the other, and if you only indulge in what's safe and secure, in protecting the comfort zones of the individual, weighing measurable professional competences over diversity, you will create an organization which is likely to excel at constant optimization and quality improvement of already existing products and services. However, an organization reaching for radical or disruptive innovation – finding unknown solutions to hitherto unknown problems – needs to nurture the individual freedom and creativity, diversity, and incompetence, and to allow for a certain degree of chaos. Furthermore, the potential of not knowing must be taken seriously, and admitting one's ignorance needs to be both respected and encouraged. If ignorance, incompetence, and chaos is not acknowledged as resources, then the barrier for taking risks will be too high for most individuals. Radical innovation requires that both incompetence and a certain degree of chaos are embraced. This point of view, by the way, is also shared by the CEO of the world's most successful design agency, IDEO, the previously referred to Tim Brown, who also is known for preaching that "Innovation requires willingness to embrace chaos."

Another interesting angle on innovation and enhancing an organization's innovation capacity is to look at its "excess capacity," hidden in the midst of the organization and embodied by its members of staff. This capacity is fairly easily accessible, provided a corporate culture truly encourages it to surface. The founder of the successful manufacturer of cabinets and storage systems Montana, Peter Lassen has said that "The individual member of our team – from the CEO to the maintenance assistance is

---

[12]O. Brafman and J. Pollack. (2013). *The Chaos Imperative – How Chance and Disruption Increase Innovation, Effectiveness, and Success* (New York, NY: Penguin Random House).

part of Montana's design team – our design is renewed every time a new member of staff is recruited."[13]

Nobody knows a company's products or processes or a public administration's service to its community better than the company's own staff or the public service provider's own officers. They meet both the products and services, but also the suppliers and processes behind them, and the receivers and users at the front. Hence, nobody is better suited to contribute with valuable input than them, to be found at both hands of the transaction. Many of them just don't know it themselves, and are rarely encouraged to dig down into the valuable reservoir of knowledge they possess.

A corporate culture which encourages its individuals on all levels and regardless of their direct role in and responsibility for product, service, or business development to take part and contribute actively to development and change processes will gradually build an advanced degree of "innoliteracy" – knowledge about of understanding of how innovation happens, all the way from the CEO and down to the individual CNC operator or caretaker – a recognition of the excess capacity, thus latent innovation capacity that most organizations dispose of through the knowledge and experiences vested in their staff.

It does require, of course, that each individual member of staff is introduced to what innovation is and why it is important, and granted the trust and confidence that each and every one can contribute to creating innovation at their own workplace or whatever environment they are part of. And perhaps, most of all, it requires a common understanding of the fact that "good ideas couldn't care less who got them."

Innovation is rarely radical – only very few have the gift and the conditions to come up with transformational solutions. But less can do; even small, incremental improvements are valuable, and just as much innovation as the game-changing kind that hits the front pages of *Time* and *Newsweek*. Therefore, it does not necessarily take specialized knowledge on innovation as a process, about models and methodologies to contribute to valuable development and change. What it takes, though, is that

---

[13]P. Lassen. CEO of the Danish furniture manufacturer, Montana, in an article by Wood Industry in 2008.

this knowledge either exists in the organization, or that someone in the organization acknowledges the value of and is qualified to procure such expertise externally; people who can facilitate, manage, and moderate creative processes.

There is, however, a fundamental assumption for contributing to such processes of innovation and change, and that is to be invited and respected for one's capacity to do so. This requires, as previously mentioned, an organizational or corporate culture that embraces the individual and what he or she brings to the table on his or her own terms. If one succeeds in doing so, however, the door to new knowledge, which has been hidden under one's nose for ages, is opened, and some of the dogmas and "truths" that often build up in closed environments are suddenly being dismantled.

This is not about filling staff members with hot air, but simply a matter of granting the individual the reassurance that they actually possess valuable knowledge and experience, which can contribute to the organization's development and well-being, and which nobody else has. Then, the understanding of how the game is played and where the individual has the most to offer slowly grows at his or her own pace.

The path toward a genuinely creative organization – with creative staff and creative leadership – can be long and bumpy, and an organization characterized by a mind-set and true understanding of how to work creatively as a rule and not as an exception does not come by itself. Fortunately, a solid base of research and empirical evidence of how one systematically builds such a culture – including how the individual's creative potential is released – and how creative and collaborative processes are introduced in an organization already exists. One quite accessible, and for most corporate leaders, quite recognizable model is developed by the Swiss researcher Claudia Acklin.[14] She considers the journey toward an organization embracing managed creative processes as a cultural battle, where one or more individuals in the organization believing in and possibly having own previous experiences of working with creative processes, often

---

[14]C. Acklin. (2011). "Design Management Absorption Model – A Framework to Describe the Absorption Process of Design Knowledge by SME's with Little or No Prior Design Experience," *Creativity and Innovation Management* 22, pp. 147–160.

helped by external designers or other creative professionals, become front-runners and show the rest of the organization how it works by inviting them in and to give the credits for the good results it produces. Slowly and project by project, inviting in the right people – one at a time – thus slowly building confidence and enthusiasm throughout the organization, fuelled by good experiences and good results. Through this "Trojan Horse" tactics, experience shows that permission is granted to apply these new methods and techniques onto gradually larger and more complex challenges, slowly and by help of empirical evidence transforming the way that the organization relates to phenomena such as creative iterations, stakeholder engagement, and scenario prototyping.

PART 3

Scoping, Framing, and Reframing – The Best Possible Solution to the Rightest Possible Problem

According to the author of two books dedicated to the art and power of framing, in an organizational context, framing represents "the means by which leaders and students of leadership, learn to manage meaning."[1]

Professor Robert M. Entman of George Washington University[2] in his research refers to framing as "scattered conceptualization" – to choose some factors over others with the purpose of supporting an idea or favor one assessment to another – or simply to strengthen a message.

There is a quote, attributed to Albert Einstein:

> If I had an hour to solve a problem and my life depended on the solution, I would spend the first fifty-five minutes determining the proper question to ask, for once I knew the proper question, I could solve the problem in less than five minutes.

Reframing is all about "determining the proper question to ask"; about seeing a situation, challenge, or problem from as many different angles as possible. Framing *and* reframing make up the process where we, either subconsciously or in a more structured manner, assess and understand

---

[1]G.T. Fairhurst. (2011). *The Power of Framing: Creating the Language of Leadership* (Hoboken, NJ: Wiley).

[2]R.M. Entman. (1993). Framing: Toward Clarification of a Fractured Paradigm, *Journal of Communication* 43, no. 4.

what the situation or problem at hand is all about, its context, and its construct.

Once in a while, one is faced with the situation of someone, perhaps a teenage nephew or someone else with the guts to challenge one's intellectual capacity – featured at the back of a boulevard newspaper; a so-called brain-twister. The challenge is often rather banal – at least at first glance; we also know them from recruitment tests and admission tests for organizations for the gifted, or at least so, I've been told. Actually, besides a trivial pursuit, they can be quite valuable to train and encourage new ways of looking at a problem. Mostly for fun, this is one example:

The challenge is specified to connect the nine dots with a maximum of four lines without lifting the pencil from the paper, and without crossing any of the nine dots more than once.

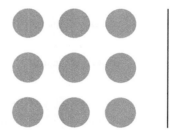

Piece of cake – again, at first glance – but often trickier than what you'd think, especially when the four lines are suddenly "used" and there is still an unconnected dot. Damn. But it forces one to think out of the box. How far outside of the dots must I go? Well, nobody put any restrictions on that, really. And nobody said that the lines had to be straight, did they?

The standard solution to the challenge, and authorized by the Danish Ministry of Education, where the test can be found, is this:

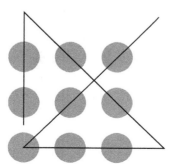

The "standard" solution shows that it is actually possible to move beyond the perimeters that we all create in our own heads, framing the nine dots. As the "authorized" and ministerial comment to the models says:

> Our personality tends to react normatively. We allow being limited by what we see on our inner screen – in this case straight lines, crossing the centre of the dot and departing equally far from the configuration on all sides etc.

– without any of those being limitations we actually need to observe.

Thus, in addition to the "authorized" solution, one could also imagine other ways of approaching the challenge, and which are equally aligned with the brief; for example, this one:

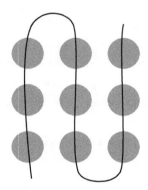

or this one

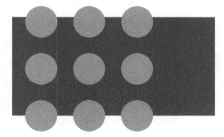

Nobody prohibited us from nor forced us to use all four lines – that was a maximum – and nobody demanded the lines to be straight or thin, so a single line, whether curved or just very fat, also solves the problem perfectly well. The Hungarian Noble Prize winner in Medicine in 1937, Albert Szengyörgyi, who received the prize for the discovery of the Vitamin C, said at the prize ceremony that "Discovery consists of looking at the same thing as everyone else and thinking something different." Fortunately, there is always someone who, just and without questions, takes things for what they are.

David Straker is a psychologist and author, focusing on problem solving and decision making, persuasion, and influence. He manages a web source called *www.changingminds.org*, which – in short – revolves around finding the best possible solution to the rightest possible problem. He explains that we instinctively frame everything around us, according to an internalized map consisting of assumptions that we never question, and which we use when decoding and making sense of what happens around us. If one element in the frame changes or is reframed, what we experience is suddenly decoded differently and changes meaning. To reframe, we need to take a step backward from what is being said or happens before us, and try to understand the situation in the context of the frame in which it is said or takes place. We also need to try to understand the tacit assumptions and motives for the situation, and by saying, "let's look at this through a different lens," we challenge the frame and can assess it more freely. One way of doing this is to question whether the situation is characterized by being a problem or an opportunity, a strength or a weakness (what we know as a SWOT analysis), if it is a situation which needs an intervention, something we simply cannot do anything about, or possibly, a mere misunderstanding.

So, the process of framing and reframing is all about establishing a relevant context for the challenge one wants to work with, to explore different perspectives, to challenge the "truth" and to influence both one's own and others' mind-set and mental state of mind in the situation. One has to introduce what Raymond Turner calls a "bias free zone" – a space where everyone is reminded that no ideas are shot down; they are all valid until discussed and put to a test. Reflection is one out of several, but possibly the most important individual tool to test whether the problem at hand – its meaning, significance, and implications – is just the most conspicuous one, hence the one our instincts would call upon us to solve. But again, there are many other approaches to put a challenge to test and to make sure that the situation is properly framed and reframed before a development or change process demanding all kinds of resources is embarked upon.

One of the reformists of Danish corporate culture, Lars Kolind, known for what was called the "spaghetti organization" when he introduced it as CEO of the global hearing aid manufacturing company Oticon in the late 1980s, had as his starting point the need to "reframe" what it takes for a company to perform better.[3]

Cutting down was not a bad thing – he compared it to pruning a fruit tree, where the branches not carrying fruit are cut away, but mostly to give more light and nutrition to those that do. I had the pleasure of taking part in a leadership camp at his private estate, where he lives and hosts leadership development programs. There, he talked a lot about "mental models." Everyone has a mental model constructed from their own professional background, organizational affinity, position and social standing, and so on. The challenge is to reframe one's own role by understanding and getting a clear picture of which model one carries, and then, reflect upon how and when it came into being, on which logic it is founded, and whether it supports the goals and objectives one has and strives toward. The same questions can be asked about one's contribution to and mental model in relation to a specific process or development project.

The Question Often Not Asked: New Development or Improvement

All organizations, just like each and every one of us as individuals, survive and blossom by being in constant movement and in constant development. As a professional organization, it is a prerequisite for survival that a strategically conceived and managed development takes place at all times – whether it focuses on organizational structures or individual competences, internal processes and routines, or on the products or

---

[3]L. Kolind. (2000). *The knowledge Society; Agenda for Denmark in the 21st Century* (Copenhagen, Denmark: Gyldendal).

services one's justification in the market depends on. And yet, one should always ask if all development is necessarily good or needed.

In principle, there are two kinds of development: the one which appears as "organic," ongoing, and subtle, and just a natural reflection of a dynamic and conscious organizational culture, where common goals and aspirations for the organization in itself is a driving force for gradual improvements, and where it neither is defined as a "project" nor managed by anyone in particular. The other kind is "strategic," conceived and managed as an integrated part of an overall plan. Both kinds most often take place in parallel, and should point in the same overall direction; otherwise, there are some serious issues to be discussed in the organization. This book focuses primarily on the latter kind; development or change through strategically conceived and managed processes related to what it is that the organization delivers or how.

When I, quite deliberately, equal change and development, and see both as results of an innovation process, it is simply because far too often, something new is developed from scratch instead of improving on something already existing. Often, solutions which fundamentally respond to a specific need already exist, whether on stock or developed to a point, where delivery can easily be done, and where rather marginal changes are needed for the solution to be marketable or to fulfill user expectations. Far too often, companies respond to falling market shares by developing a new product or service that can boost sales and revenue, while often, a slight redesign or optimization of an already existing product or service would have been a much better investment.

The question of whether to start afresh or whether to build upon something existing needs to be resolved after careful consideration and as part of the very early phases of a development process, by allocating time and resources to really get to the bottom of whether the market one operates in and the position one already has in it call for strategies to supplement existing products or services with new ones, exchanging the existing with new, or merely optimizing the already existing ones. Giving the marketplace more options does not necessarily make it either easier or more likely to choose what it is that you have to offer, and a choice between a constantly growing number of options does not make the one who has to choose more content about their choice – rather, the opposite.

In fact, research shows quite clearly that a supplier or brand often loses its grip by the user, if the number of options makes the choice too hard.[4,5]

Framing, Reframing, and Existing Process Models

Many would claim that framing and reframing are already part of the standard process model that most designers as well as organizations working with development use. Design – or problem solving, if you wish – is an iterative process, which probably explains why most graphic representations of design processes consist of circular elements. And it's true that most development processes to be found – even somewhat, and possibly unfairly generalized – roughly consist of the same stages:

- Identify the problem.
- Identify criteria and barriers.
- Generate ideas for possible solutions.
- Explore realistic scenarios.
- Choose among alternatives.
- Create a prototype.
- Test and refine.
- Produce, execute, or launch.

However, these are not necessarily a sequential process, where the individual elements come in exactly the listed order.

Equally generalized, but still valid for many larger organizations, all these "iterations" are part of an overall, linear process – more often than not a version of or inspired by the "stage-gate model," based on clearly defined milestones throughout the process. When an idea has been developed, it has to pass the first "gate" before the actual process can start. The first stage is called "scoping" or "innovation assessment"; then a gate, then a stage focusing on exploring and elaborating on the idea; and then,

[4]S. Iyengar and M. Lepper. (2000). "When Choice is Demotivating: Can one Desire Too Much of a Good Thing?," *Journal of Personality and Social Psychology* 79, no. 6, pp. 995–1006.

[5]B. Schwartz. (2004). *The Paradox of Choice – Why More Is Less* (New York, NY: Harper Perennial).

Figure 3.1 Stage-gate is developed by Dr. Robert G. Cooper and is a registered trademark owned by Product Development Institute Inc.

the next gate. If the idea is mature and passes the gate, the next stage focuses on building a business case or a "proof of concept" for further development (Figure 3.1).

After the third gate, the actual development process starts in collaboration with clients or other stakeholders, and this is where the bulk of the resources allocated are most often disposed of.

After the fourth "gate," the project enters into a testing and validation stage, before the fifth and last "gate" determines whether to launch or not. Regardless of which one out of an unknown, but extensive number of versions of the "stage-gate model" one encounters, it replicates the pattern of managing the process through a set of decision-making "locks" to ensure that resources are not wasted on a project, which at the end of the day, is not a viable proposition. It should also be mentioned that a vast majority of the organizations which have adopted Cooper's thinking have adapted the model to their own needs and worldview.

Many would also claim that framing and reframing are both natural elements in the three first phases of the process, where the problem is scoped, criteria and barriers identified, and ideas generated and prototyped. And of course, the problem and its solution are both adjusted as new insights about the problem are gathered through the search for a solution, but the purpose is rarely to challenge the problem, but rather, to make one's understanding of the problem and the first traces of a realistic solution meet.

My claim is that there are loads of arguments to choose an approach, where a relatively large portion of the available resources is allocated to the very early phases of a process. The weightiest argument to do so is not to dwell on the nitty-gritty details of the problem identified before the development process as such starts, but to make sure that it is actually the right problem we address.

The paradox, as I see it – as the two are often seen as contradictory – is that there is no contradiction at all between following a linear process, as represented by, for example, the stage-gate model and working design methodologically with its focus on exploration and excavation of underlying layers, and to "read the weak signals."

Actually, the stage-gate model does not prescribe which activities that actually take place within each individual stage, between the four (sometimes more) gates, a project has to pass. In fact, the headings more than indicate that certain iterations are implicitly part of each one of the five stages. So, from here on, my assumption is that the development process, as such, is linear and that decisions are made at crucial points in time as it moves along, and that each "stage" contains a series of iterative processes, allowing for continuous reflection and reframing.

The INNOLITERACY model is simply a proposition for those, looking for a more "organic" and "grounded" development model, on one side structured as any classic development process from A to Z, and on the other, embracing the uncertainties and unforeseen elements that wondering and questioning, reflecting, trying and failing, and welcoming input from as many different sources of inspiration as possible, add. Its overall objective is to open up for deeper insights and a more profound understanding of the problem itself as well as those for whom a solution is developed.

I personally do not believe in simple and unambiguous methods, often presented as "quick fixes," and I question the value of any attempt to reduce a complex issue to a simple drawing, graph, or formula as if there were any shortcut to meaningful innovation. This book goes against the trend, as such, as it sort of presupposes that the reader has the time and interest to actually read it – not from cover to cover at once, I think it tastes much better in small portions – and that he or she takes the inspiration it hopefully offers back into their own organizations and day-to-day operations, and into the processes where future development activities are planned and resources allocated. All that said, I had to realize as I worked with the material, that a graphic representation of my thinking to organize its elements and to accentuate its focus on reflection and reframing was inevitable.

Framing, Reframing, and Demands on Method and Structure

Up until now, the whole concept of reflection has been the most crucial individual element in a process, more than anything focusing on the current situation to make sure that the energy is directed toward solving the right problem. I have also tried to describe the conditions needed to allow an organization and its management to access all available, valuable sources of contributions to it. I will revert to both of these "inhibitions" as we move on, but for now, I will divert my focus from the individual, the subject, to the model framework wherein the process takes place.

So-called creative processes are often challenged in environments focusing on increasingly fierce demands for measurable ROI for each single decision, operation, or approach as a result of LEAN processes, productivity benchmarks, or demands for austerity. And as such, there is pretty good evidence supporting that creativity in itself does not create much value in an organization. Research shows that investment in design in itself is no guarantee of better performance, unless the design process is integrated into the overall strategies of the organization and managed with the same stringency and demands for accountability as any other process taking place within the organization.[6]

Design management is perhaps the best example of a structured approach to managing creative processes, as design is the individual creative discipline, which to the greatest extent, has found its way into commercial as well as not-for-profit organizations as an approach to accommodating needs for change and development. Based on the rather extensive literature on design management produced up through the 1980s, the 1990s, and the 2000s, we now have systematically generated and documented knowledge on how to benefit the most from processes, where design and designers play a key role. In brevity and perhaps unjustly simplified, the research shows that the benefits are directly correlated with the degree of strategic anchoring and management support, multidisciplinarity and extensive stakeholder engagement, and

---

[6]A. Fernández-Mesa, J. Alegre-Vidal, R. Chiva-Gómez, and A. Gutiérrez-Gracia. (2012). "Design Management Capability and Product Innovation in SMEs," *Management Decision* 51, no. 3, pp.547–565.

with design processes being managed with the same prudence and professionalism as any other key area for the organization – be it digitization or human resource development or the building of a new domain.

I have earlier referred to Cooper's stage-gate model as a very common, and in most cases, extremely useful basis model for development of new products, services, and systems. At the same time, its basic structure is so simple that most organizations using it have revised it to be more targeted and to fit more immediately into the individual organization's own structure and understanding. Moreover, at the same time as being linear, it has proven quite clearly that it does not necessarily hamper an organization's creativity. One of the most successful and creative companies of all times, LEGO, work with stage-gate as a fundamental process management tool, alongside and integrated with its own design development processes.[7]

A recently undertaken project, cofinanced by the EU – European House of Design Management (EHDM)[8] – a project in which I was deeply involved over a 3-year period explores and aims at facilitating the transfer of successful design management and stakeholder engagement strategies from private sector design and innovation-driven companies to the public sector, thus helping the sector to absorb design thinking and design methodologies as a relevant management tool when developing new public services. Also, this project has shown that it is necessary to observe linearity and stage-by-stage logics to resonate with how public services are both developed and delivered and the value chain that a public service provider is part of. Also in the EHDM project, the process skeleton clearly resembles the classic "stage-gate" model. The major difference lies in much heavier focus on audits, revisions, and validation as integrated elements of the development process itself, and built-in "loopholes" allowing extra iterations back to the exploration phase (Figure 3.2).

---

[7] *"LEGO's Innovation model is integrated in our development process, which in our case is a classical stage-gate process in 12-month cycles."* Mike Ganderton, Creative Senior Director - Product and Marketing Development.

[8] European House of Design Management was one out of six projects funded by the EU's *"1st Action Plan of the European Design Innovation Initiative Action no: ENT/ CIP/11C/N03C021."* The project ran from 2012 to 2015 and materialized in the web resource SHAPE – www.shapebetterservices.eu

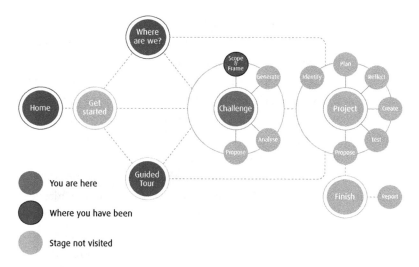

Figure 3.2 European House of Design Management's development model, as it appears in the "SHAPE" resource

However, to revert to the original stage-gate model, I have chosen to start my journey with sticking to the five "stages" and tried to give them names, which are slightly more "generic" than the original, thus more accommodating to my attempt at building a higher degree of reflection, framing, and reframing into the process, and to work with more precisely articulated problems. The original terms are the ones in brackets. Moreover, I have deliberately removed the last "gate" – and I'll get back to why that is when we get there (Figure 3.3).

However, the significance in changing the words is not the words themselves, just like the elements are rather parallel. The significance lies in introducing terms, which do not restrict us to development and launch of commercial products (even though we all know that a product can also be immaterial, most of tends to attach it to something coming out of a machine), but also to allow for the model to be applied to services, systems, and organizational changes. Another reason for challenging the terminology is to allow for a different allocation of resources than what the original model indicates. In general terms, my thinking calls for much more focus on and resources allocated to stages one and two, and for me, the second gate is far too early to make final decisions – at this stage, we're still trying to understand which problem it is that we end up actually solving.

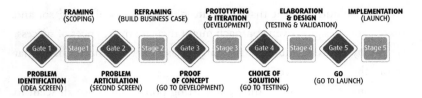

Figure 3.3 *My own, slightly modified version of Cooper's stage-gate model*

Fundamentally speaking, I believe that the model has deserved such universal appeal because it focuses on developing products faster and more efficiently and with more market relevance, and who could be against that? My claim, though, is that the same approach can be used to develop better solutions to problems in general by understanding the problem better.

At this stage, I have to clarify that I'm by far the first one to describe how design methodology and stage-gate thinking can coexist. One of the most recognized researchers and advocates for design management, the French professor Brigitte Borja de Mozota,[9] in her book *Design Management – Using Design to Build Brand Value and Corporate Innovation*, which is standard curriculum for anyone studying design management, also uses Cooper's model as a starting point, and then, adds the activities normally being part of a design process. Her contribution is inevitable and highly relevant even after more than a decade, and has been a vital source of inspiration for my further processing and thinking.

My contribution is by no means a rebellion against – or even criticism of – Cooper's model. I will merely use it as a vehicle to further develop my own thinking, coming from design as an untapped potential, provided the process is managed as professionally as any other process in an organization, and as a mental framework for how a different approach to how any organization's three key resources, time, people, and budgets, can be balanced differently from what we see in most organizations today. And as such, I'm totally on the same page as Cooper – to develop faster, more efficiently, and with better chances of success in the marketplace,

---

[9]B. Borja de Mozota. (2003). *Design Management – Using Design to Build Brand Value and Corporate Innovation* (New York, NY: Allworth Press).

and merely adding to it that there are different ways of doing so, and that a more design-driven approach might increase the chances of success, simply by focusing more on the early phases of the process than what most other models describe.

I could have chosen a different starting point, but as we all seem to relate quite intuitively to linear thinking and models, and as Cooper's model is already part of most organizations' methodical portfolio, it just seemed like a good place to start. And in any case, we will soon move on to what is actually novel in the INNOLITERACY approach.

At the end of the day, the most important is that a model and structure for development is found, which supports and fits the decision-making processes and how other processes are managed in the organization – partly to enhance the project's own chances of success, but even more importantly, to make sure that it supports overall corporate strategies or, for that matter, the political ambitions for a local, regional, or national government.

On an operational level, the more important issue is to dispose of the resources available in the most effective manner possible within the chosen structure. And that's what I will dwell on in the next section of the book, a discussion "stage" by "stage" and "gate" by "gate" – moving slowly toward a model which goes beyond de Mozota's schematic merger of stage-gate and design, and which is not, at least not to the same degree, confined to the revenue-focused parameters known in the corporate world.

Fuzzy Front End

In the jungle of buzzwords we encounter in our innovation hungry age of time, "fuzzy front end" is one of the more interesting. The term is used about the very early and often a little messy idea generation phase, perfectly portrayed in Damien Newman's "squiggle," as you find in the preface of this book. This is the phase that I will focus on and encourage, that we all pay more attention to. Many have done so before me, and there is already quite a lot of literature and research devoted to it, describing the correlation between what our focus is at the outset of a project and the project outcome. The two researchers, Cornelius Herstatt and Birgit Verworn[10] find that there is a direct correlation between the success rates of innovation projects on the one hand and the attention to and willingness to invest in the *fuzzy front end*. Moreover, an empirical study made by Cooper and Kleinschmidt as early as in 1988 supports that "high failure rates have often been related to insufficiencies, low management attention and poor financial support during the 'fuzzy front end.'"[11]

So, much indicates that it is in the very early, foggy phases that the most interesting propositions as to which problem to actually solve are found, and where radically new solutions are born; here, where the process is not yet clearly defined and where the curiosity still is stronger than the urge to find the final answer. This is where the response to any given problem could still be a new method, a new service, a new product, or a new technology . . .

This is where the next-generation experience, economy, or welfare society is challenged. This is where designers in union with all kinds of other creative souls can think big ideas, elaborate into scenarios, and draft a future not yet defined. And this is where one understands what the real problem is. There is only one downside about this extremely fascinating space. Even though more than a decade has passed since the quoted findings were published, nothing much has happened to act on them. The organizations are still few and far between, which actually prioritize something "fuzzy" enough to actually unlock new perspectives on how we deal with a problem – in ways that nobody ever thought about before.

Many companies allocate both time and substantial budgets to future studies, and to forecast the role and potential of their products or technologies in a future and not yet existing market environment and competitive situation. But there's often a limit to how fuzzy one can expect a company to be. If it excels at producing microchips for computers, the

---

[10]C. Herstatt and B. Verworn. (2004). "The 'Fuzzy Front End' of Innovation" In *Bringing Technology and Innovation into the Boardroom*, edited by EITIM. New York, NY: Palgrave MacMillan.

[11]R.C. Cooper and E.J. Kleinschmidt. (1988). "Resource Allocation in the New Product Process," *Industrial Marketing Management* 17, no. 3, pp. 249–262.

discussion will most probably revolve around new and yet not existing applications of microchips – or possibly what its successor will be. One would probably not be voted employee of the week if one's proposition were to look at something really low-tech. Or if an employee of a concrete-based building firm suddenly started exploring the constructive potentials of bamboo.

So, the challenge is partly to take out as much fuzziness of the fuzzy front end as is needed to be given the necessary resources, and partly to make sure that the energy going into it is perceived relevant by those endorsing it (Figure 3.4).

A Closer Look at the Individual Phases of the INNOLITERACY Model

Let's get back to the model for a moment. Every iteration – and from here on, I will refer to it as a round, as most of us can relate to that – consists of several elements. The process consists of four rounds, each round producing an output, which will be fed into the following decision-making gate.

As an example that I will refer to again and again, I have chosen a hypothetical and yet very real and serious challenge shared by most parts of the Western world – the alarmingly increasing degree of obesity among children and youngsters. I could have chosen many other examples from the private or the public sector, but have chosen this particular one because of its transversal relevance, because of its complexity, and because no one seems to have found a viable approach to how to deal with it yet. And because I personally experienced the consequences of being overweight as a child and teenager, and I know which scars it leaves on a young person's soul – scars that I would wish that others were spared.

Understanding the Problem

Regardless of which method is applied, the very first phase in the process should be to identify and understand the problem, a fundamental prerequisite for any meaningful later rounds with the objective of solving what we then agree on being the right problem.

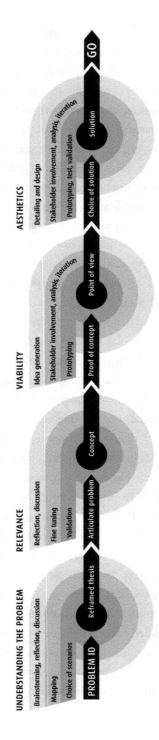

Figure 3.4 The INNOLITERACY model

The process starts with ideas and reflections, data, and whatever makes us believe that there is a challenge to be addressed being fed into the "system," where it is all being discussed, sorted, and challenged. In many companies – probably also in many other forms of organizations – mechanisms to make sure that such input is reported to the relevant person or department is built into quality assurance systems or other procedures. Other organizations don't, but the key issue at this stage is to identify which problem to address or whether it actually is a challenge to embark upon or not – regardless of whether it has been reported as one among many problems, based on user or operator feedback, whether it has been spotted as part of a strategy process, prompted by legislation or budget cuts, or simply by someone having a brilliant idea. And the problem or challenge can be of a nature, which is addressed by developing something new or improving on something already existing, be it a product, a service, an activity, or a physical space – or an instruction or legislation, for that matter. In any case, whether a problem, a challenge, or just an interesting venture, I have chosen the heading "understanding the problem" as the first thing for which some kind of consensus needs to be established. This is to ensure that among all the possible initiatives one could take, the "problem" most likely to give return on investment – no matter how ROI is measured – is the one addressed. This, however, is not the same as concluding that the problem is the most crucial one; it only means that a choice has been made, possibly among many other and equally interesting ones, and that a project has been called.

Then, some would say, "OK, so far so good, but we haven't really got any further, then, have we . . .?" And the answer to that is Yes, because you have started and framed a process, and you have started a conversation. You have identified an area of concern, where everyone agrees that there is room for improvement. For example, within public health care, there may be hundreds of challenges "someone" ought to do something about – from obesity, smoking, and alcoholism via reproduction issues to growing numbers of elderly with Alzheimer's disease or an explosive increase in repetitive strain injuries among school children. However, if "one" happens to be a regional government with a limited budget for preventive and proactive initiatives to improve the general well-being of one's citizens, choices have to be made. It could – just as an example – be to address the previously introduced problem of obesity among children of the ages 10 to 15.

In Denmark, according to the National Health Agency, from being a problem for one out of a thousand children in the 1950s, 10 percent of all children of that age group today struggle with weight problems, and it's even worse in certain other industrialized countries. So, a problem has been identified – one among many, but one for which there is both public and political support to take a closer look at.

It sounds easy enough to get to that point, but it is not always a road without bumps. To start with, we're dealing with an area, and we're still looking at public health, just not to confuse anyone, where there is almost no end to the issues one could potentially address, and where the source of information about dysfunctions, and of opinions about what to prioritize, are plentiful. There is the public opinion, there are health care professionals on all levels – from hands-on experience in care institutions or hospitals to national players such as patient organizations or unions, researchers and lifestyle opinion-makers, media and a range of industries profiting from other people's problems, from pharmaceuticals to assistive technologies. And just because knowledge exists does not mean that it is easily available or – if it is – that it is trustworthy. In particular, statistical knowledge gathered among civilians is often more a reflection of self-staging than of real life. As an example, a Danish national survey from 2012, developed to map the consumption of cultural experiences and products, showed that the Danes had been to the theatre 9.3 million times during the year. During the same period, the national statistical bureau figures show that 1.9 million theatre tickets were sold – quite exactly 20 percent of what the respondents had claimed. In other words, 80 percent of the respondents, saying that they had been to the theatre in the past year, lied. Probably for a number of different reasons, but the truth it certainly wasn't.

So, whom do we listen to and what is the quality of the information on which we act? How do we end up with a situation where everyone agrees that the obesity among 10- to 15-year-olds is the right one to focus on? Why not arthritis or diabetes among middle-aged women or ADHD or autism among preschool boys in particular? And how do we feel somewhat reassured that the insights we gather actually reflect the wishes and worries of the whole, selected target group and that they are truly motivated to be part of a solution?

One thing that we never seem to run out of is "wicked problems"[12] – problems of such complexity that most solutions would interfere with existing structures and risk creating new and unknown problems of an unknown magnitude. So, the fact of the matter is that the choice of which problem to address is often motivated by a combination of how sturdy the knowledge at hand seems to be, pressure from all kinds of interests and their lobbyists and advocates, and of which problems seem the most realistic to solve within a reasonable time frame and realistic means. In one of his books about public sector innovation, Christian Bason refers to an article by the researcher Gambhir Bhatta in *The Innovation Journal*, claiming that there is evidence that the more "wicked" or complicated a problem seems to be, the less likely it is that any public sector body will ever run the risks of addressing it.[13,14]

If we now give ourselves the benefit of doubt and say that we do not always instinctively take the easy way out, and let us assume that both public and private sector managers choose their challenges based on importance, and not on x-factor, then tools to measure importance is necessary, but importance in relation to what? As for the health care sector, importance can be measured in savings on public sector budgets, possible improvements of the life quality, or life expectancy of the individual citizen, what could have been achieved elsewhere with the same resources, and of course, seen in relation to the resources it would actually take.

Already here, it would be beneficial and sometimes decisive to embark on the challenge that a structured and focused analysis is undertaken, where the problem is framed in detail, that the complexity of the situation is unveiled, and where the situation is explored to find out whether this is the real and underlying problem or a symptomatic one, and whether solving another or other related problems could possibly be more effective.

---

[12]C.W. Churchman. (1967). "Wicked Problems," *Management Science* 14, no. 4.

[13]C. Bason. (2010). *Leading Public Sector Innovation – Co-creating for a better society* (Bristol, UK: Policy Press).

[14]G. Bhatta. (2003). "Don't Just Do Something, Stand There! Revisiting the Issue of Risks in Innovation in the Public Sector" *The Innovation Journal* 8, no. 2.

Some approaches, which have proven useful for others, and in the private sector in particular, could possibly also inspire problem-solving processes both in the public and the third sector. One of them is W. Chan Kim and Renée Mauborgne's "Blue Ocean Strategy"[15] and the other is Clayton Christensen's "Disruptive Innovation."[16] Both theories deals with finding solutions which do not only solve any given problem, but which are radically different in their outlook, either by finding solutions, where no comparable or parallel references exist, or by solving problems never addressed before.

An often referred-to example is the Canadian Cirque de Soleil, which by eliminating the two biggest cost factors of running a circus – animals and expensive stars – and at the same time, redefining the market from kids bringing their parents to an adult and discriminating audience, revolutionized the entire concept of circus. The two founders, Guy Laliberté and Daniel Gauthier, both previous street artists, now reign over a global brand with an approximate 3,500 staff and a turnover of more than half a billion dollars.

Back to our obesity challenge, we now choose to believe that a thorough analysis exists, as do the best intentions ever, justifying that some kind of action needs to be taken to fight the rapidly growing number of 10- to 15-year-old kids, who are either overweight, severely overweight, or obese. The decision is made, as it – on short term – will contribute to better life quality and less problems related to social relations, inclusion, and bullying for the individual on the one hand, and more pragmatically, to reduced costs due to a decrease in needs for symptom treatment in the primary health care sector, on the other. Moreover, there are long-term medical and health care political arguments to address the problem, partly related to the individual's lifetime expectancy and partly related to the expectancy of overweight and obese people being a lifelong burden on the

---

[15]W.C. Kim and R. Mauborgne. (2005). *Blue Ocean Strategy: How to Create Uncontested Market Space and Make Competition Irrelevant"* (Boston, MA: Harvard Business School Press).

[16]C. Christensen. (1997). *The Innovator's Dilemma; When New Technologies Cause Great Firms to Fail* (Boston, MA: Harvard Business Review Press).

public health care system. So, the initiative can be argued both politically, economically, medically, and from a humanistic perspective.

In this particular example, one could imagine that there would be several open questions, such as on which level the most efficient initiatives would be taken and coordinated – whether locally, regionally, or nationally. Let us now assume that this process is anchored nationally after an initiative from the Ministry of Health, and that a certain amount of money has been allocated in the ministry's budget, while the actual activities in principle can be decentralized and shared between the three levels. I make this assumption because it fits into the rationale of this book, but also because we're dealing with an issue which probably needs to be addressed on all three levels to deliver successful results, in any case. And because it describes an almost ideal condition to start with such an open mandate, and then, to design the solution from an effectiveness angle instead of what could often be the case – to design disconnected initiatives to fit predefined budgetary and bureaucratic premises.

So, we're looking at a nationally initiated and financed campaign to "do something about" the fact that more and more kids end up as overweight or obese, and it is still up in the air how we dispose of the budgets at hand. Why is that important? Well, to me, it is because in a Danish context, at least, a grant to regional governments would have meant that the initiative would be anchored and implemented as a health care initiative – that's what the Danish regions are responsible for – give or take. At least 96 percent of their budgets go to hospitals and other health care facilities. On the other hand, if the initiative were to be anchored locally, the implementation would be developed to take place in schools or youth clubs or municipal libraries, or a combination of the above. And if the grant were to be disposed of and implemented by the ministry itself or the National Health Agency, the result would most probably be another app. It is quite puzzling how many problems we seem to believe that we can solve by either developing another web portal or a website, or – as a more recent alternative – an app. The question is whether "another" digital facility in itself solves anything at all in itself. My best answer to that would be a No.

Of course, the public sector, just like the private sector and NGOs, networks and associations, families and individuals, should take full advantage of the fantastic possibilities that the digital development has given and constantly offers us. According to the Danish Ministry of Economics and Internal Affairs, the public sector in Denmark will save a 120 million Euros annually when the government's target of 80 percent of the dialogue between the individual and the "system" happens via digital self-service. That is significant and shouldn't be dismissed. The question, though, is whether the transaction of knowledge or information taking place digitally between the citizen and the system – if it is allowed to stand on its own – serves the intended purpose. In any case, a fundamental prerequisite for embarking on a project of such a magnitude and complexity as any project involving so many parties and concerns on the side of the sender and affecting so many individuals on the side of the receiver is, that one really knows the problem at stake quite intimately.

Framing and Reframing

Framing and reframing are central to this book, as they, seen in isolation, are the most important building blocks, and as a whole, the most significant premise for all subsequent endeavors at delivering against a precisely defined and relevant goal. When the problem has been properly identified, it makes a whole lot of sense to rewind and ask once again, so are we now sure that we are solving the right problem? As Albert Einstein said, it wasn't that he was so much smarter than others, he just dwelled a little longer on each challenge. It's not that we go back and ask whether the problem identified really is a problem, but whether it is the most relevant to solve first. There is no question that far too many kids between 10 and 15 weigh too much; whether a little, some, or much too much – it is a problem, and that problem has a range of negative consequences, both short term and long term. The danger is that we start looking for solutions to a problem that is so complex that it cannot be dealt with by doing one thing. The result would be that the response to the problem is the aforementioned app – that's how you communicate with young people, isn't it? Or, you end up by dictating more gym classes in the third to seventh grades – physical movement prevents obesity, right? Or, by . . .

Which brings us back to C. West Churchman's background for introducing the term "wicked problems" – and they can be truly wicked – that any one single solution can solve a singular problem, and at the same time, reinforce or create others.

Framing in this specific context means to take two steps back and look at the phenomenon of being overweight or obesity in all the contexts where it can be observed and contextualized. The problem is mapped, literally, by plotting into a coherent representation all the individual factors, which may have or with certainty have an influence on the existence of this as a problem. Having mapped all these factors gives birth to a number of new questions – questions which need to be dealt with one way or another, through analysis, discussion, or reflection. Is the problem one that can reasonably be seen in isolation? Is it just a symptom of other, even wickeder problems? Should it be dealt with by designating one or a limited number of concrete initiatives or activities, or would it be wiser to dig a little deeper and see if the problem would solve itself or at least be positively affected, provided other and possibly more profound problems are addressed?

In our example, chosen in part because of its wonderful complexity, it almost goes without saying that there are multiple factors causing obesity, both for the chosen age group and for the population at large. One could possibly and quite easily identify at least a handful of determining factors, such as the already indicated level of structured and systematic physical activity and how physical activity in general is stimulated among youngsters. There is the consumption of food and beverages, both with regard to quantity and quality of nutrition. There is the general pattern of activity – not the one that makes you sweat, but just one's day-to-day behavior. There is the self-esteem and the extent to which the individual is comfortable with him or herself, with friends and family, with school and after-school activities. I guess nobody today would underestimate the correlation between general well-being and the wish to also be able to take care of one's own body and physique. And then, there is the individual's understanding of how all these factors play together, of *what* actually influences on their bodies' development, and how *they* can make a difference. And then, of course, there are genetic issues and there are socioeconomic issues.

Where does one start? Where is the most likely return on investment to be harvested? Which cause-and-effect factors are the most conspicuous? When, by the way, is a child overweight and when is intervention needed? How much is caused by the individual's genes and how much is environmental? What is a result of social and peer influence, and what is a result of the individual's own social and intellectual disposition? If the bag is opened, there are goodies enough for all and for many interesting project meetings, for several brainstorming sessions, and for hours of desk research. Which, by the way, is good, as it shows that the problem in question is being taken seriously.

Understanding the Problem via Brainstorming, Reflection, and Discussion

The challenge at this point is not to "explode" the problem and sit back with a pile of unrelated fragments and questions, even though a truly coherent picture is too much to ask already now. This is the stage in the process, where the findings so far and the problem as it now stands can be discussed among people with different professional angles and seen through different lenses. Exploring the problem requires a certain amount of fragmentation, but in a manner which contributes to each angle and each fragment pointing toward the same understanding of what the challenge is. Otherwise, it will be impossible to weigh and prioritize all the alternative approaches in the next round.

Giving oneself and each other time to reflect upon and discuss the various parts of the problem complex and any other relevant factors – measured by one or more team members perceiving it as being so – is a fundamental precondition for applying design methodology to a challenge like this. This round is all about opening up and understanding the problem through reflection, brainstorming, and discussions. The same brainstorming methods as many have grown used to in later stages of the process can be applied, such as IDEO's *The Rules of Brainstorming* – available at their open web resource, *openideo.com*. The main principle is that no ideas should be dismissed; there might be an interesting potential in the most surprising input, regardless of whether the source is the CEO or the maintenance assistant in the organization.

Another interesting approach is Edward de Bono's *Six Thinking Hats*.[17] This tool revolves around different members of the team taking on different roles in the discussion of a problem – one role at the time – thus being encouraged to activate one's own both naïve and critical, rational, and emotional angles and concerns. At this stage, the key objective is to get a holistic and comprehensive understanding of the problem, hence also every conceivable angle up on the table, or, rather more often, on the wall. In terms of exploiting this phase to its utmost, it is a good idea to consider whether an external facilitator or moderator should be hired, or whether one has anyone in-house with a sufficiently "neutral" position, and yet, the skills to manage the process. What is important is that all agree on the rules and name of the game, and that the process is managed with deep respect for every single team member, so that it is not a question of whoever shouts the loudest wins the argument.

Mapping

The time is now right to start mapping and organizing all relevant elements of the problem, which individually have been identified as being possible points of entry to a project or to addressing the overall problem complex. For each element, key stakeholders are identified and relations between individual elements and various stakeholders are mapped. A practical way of dealing with this is to cluster all the post-it notes that you most probably worked with in the past phase (it may be a work-related deficiency on my side, but I take it for granted that one works with post-it notes in the brainstorming phase – as does IDEO, by the way), so that post-it notes with related concerns or related ideas are placed in groups. Having done that, the challenge is to find the internal relations between the angles, how they either support or exclude each other, and then, to do the same with the stakeholder cluster.

As with regard to looking at the internal relations between either the angles or the stakeholder clusters, it can be valuable to look at existing theories and the knowledge we have about networks. Two individuals can have one relation. It can change as time goes by or from minute to minute,

---

[17]E. De Bono. (1985). *Six Thinking Hats* (Boston, MA: Little, Brown and Company).

but if the relation exists between the two only, there is, in principle, only one relation. Three people can – altogether – have four relations, while four people can have eleven different relations. While you can see the explanation from the model underneath, it doesn't necessarily explain why this should be relevant here. Well, it is, because the same that goes for people also goes for ideas or problems. By seeing two or three or more problems in combination, new angles will appear automatically, and often angles, which could not possibly be identified by looking at the problems individually. These new angles can be instrumental in getting to the "core" of the problem or to identifying in which combination of problems the most interesting potential for a solution can be found (Figure 3.5).

In other words, if you cluster two problems, you will be able to identify a third problem as a combination of the two. If you cluster three problems, in addition to those, you will be able to see four new problems deriving from the relations between them. And if you cluster four problems, they will spur eleven new combinations, so that you suddenly have fifteen points of view. Five gives 31 in all and six gives a whole lot – just don't go there. This exercise aims at achieving clarity and precision – not confusion. However, if used wisely, it illustrates, but also helps see through the complexity that a thorough analysis creates, and as a tool to establish a frame of reference for all involved and for everyone to understand the, diversity of approaches to any given problem, it is very valuable – beyond

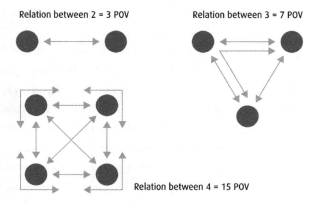

Figure 3.5 Own model inspired by Professor John Wood, Emeritus Professor of Design at Goldsmiths College, University of London. **POV = Points of View**

inevitably causing a number of good discussions and food for thought. Just be aware of the fact that this part of the process takes time, and that the process needs to be managed well to make sure that it all doesn't come to a halt, and that nothing comes out at the end.

In Cooper's model, the second stage, the one I named "reframing" in the original model called "business case," a commonly used term in the private sector. As the process I'm describing has a wider scope than a purely commercial one, I have deliberately chosen not to use the term. However relevant both in corporate life and other contexts, where a financial assessment is key, I fear that it could possibly create a barrier, vis-à-vis development communities where the objectives are not regarded as or primarily driven by pecuniary concerns.

Scenarios

As part of "framing" something, at one point – and the time has now arrived – scenarios have to be either approved or dismissed: is this something we want to pursue or not? The price of opening up for as many possible combinations of problems, approaches, and possibilities is that it takes time, and it entails a sometimes delicate process of elimination of otherwise good ideas. The upside is that the problem – after the process of opening up, discussing, and reflecting upon possible approaches – is quite likely a more relevant one than the one you started with, which in turn, is the most significant singular factor for harvesting a better return on investment at the end of the day.

Anyway, choices have to be made. It can be done in many different ways and by engaging many different players. While engaging users has hopefully already been done to the extent possible, at least at this stage, they are an obvious resource. I would invite young people, 10- to 15-year-olds, overweight as well as kids of ideal body mass, parents, and teachers, but also some of those who might already have passed the crucial age we're focusing on, and who know what it means for studies and career choices to be overweight. Talk to them, let them talk with each other while observing the relations being played out, let them discuss and solve problems together, and let them prioritize and comment on the ideas and scenarios which have been developed so far.

Some project managers would prefer to wait for such direct user intervention until the next phase, but I cannot really see how that should improve the process, except from possibly saving some time. Anyway, at one point before the problem to be solved is finally defined and articulated, relevant stakeholders for whom the problem already is, and its solution or solutions would be of great importance, need to be engaged. Anything else would be close to irresponsible, if you truly believe that having a deep understanding of the problem and of what still needs to be discovered is important to deliver a quality solution.

Making choices at this stage neither means that you choose the only problem to solve or the only solution to pursue. It merely means that we limit the number to one, which is operationally manageable. Based on our mapping and the following analysis of possible problem combinations, a limited number of scenarios – for example, three – is chosen. According to Wikipedia, a scenario is "a possible set of future events," and according to Webster's unabridged, "a description of what could possibly happen". One could also call them "theses." One thesis could be to address the quality of the food that the young kids have access to at or in the near proximity of the school and the lack of interesting, healthier alternatives. Another thesis could be to address the unsafe conditions and lack of dedicated facilities for pedestrians in the vicinity of the school, prohibiting responsible parents from sending their kids to school on their own, either by foot or bicycle, entailing that the kids are transported to and from school by car. And, a third thesis could be the body- and perfection-focused culture often dominating schools and after-school activities, causing kids who do not see themselves as "perfect" simply give up and devote themselves to computer games, soda pops, and sweets, instead of engaging in competitive, physically demanding activities. There could be many others; these three are quite arbitrarily chosen and merely reflect some of my own observations and possibly lack of knowledge. However, this book is about methodology – not about obesity.

Articulating a Thesis for Which Problem to Solve

The process and the insights gathered both from desk studies and discussions, idea generation, and user engagement sessions may point toward one of the three problems, but they may also point toward two of them or even to all three being addressed as an integrated process. We don't really know yet, and therefore, need to engage in an exercise to scrutinize and validate the three theses. Most probably, numerous factors speak in favor of, and others speak against each one of the three. Thus, we need to find out exactly which stakeholders each of the three scenarios would involve, and which support a successful resolution would require and which resistance one could expect. Possibly, or ideally, some of these have already been involved in the process thus far, and if so, some of the barriers might already have been taken care of. If not, this is the last call to invite users and other stakeholders to play a meaningful part in the process.

Besides the already mentioned and freely available methods offered by IDEO, there are a lot of interesting tools and methods out there, from which one could draw valuable inspiration. One could, for example, study the acknowledged MIT professor, Eric von Hippel's idea to democratize innovation by engaging and recognizing users as experts or "lead users," which is the term that von Hippel uses.[18] The Kolding Design School uses the terminology "experts on their own lives," but the expertise can also be on a more defined and less demanding object than one's own life. One could use IT amateur geeks to develop new software or amateur chefs to develop new kitchen utensils.

Another question is whether one or more of the scenarios raise conflicts of interest – either vis-à-vis other projects or initiatives or simply others who see things differently. A potential conflict of interest may not be decisive of whether or not to pursue an idea or scenario, but at least it's valuable to know in advance if it seems likely that you will encounter resistance.

The question of resources will have to be raised: what will the three scenarios require of time, money, and human resources, and does this favor one over the others? Are the right structures and tools in place to pursue anyone of the three scenarios, or will one or more of them require disproportional investments or changes in the organization to be successfully undertaken? Or, could it possibly be that one of the scenarios poses

---

[18]E. von Hippel (1986): "Lead Users: A Source of Novel Product Concepts," *Management Science* 32, no. 7, pp. 791–805.

a challenge, which is exactly the opportunity you have been waiting for to make an organizational castling?

Perhaps, already now, one scenario seems to be more realistic or likely to succeed than the two other, or perhaps one of the three scenarios seems to start wobbling.

Choosing "the Right Problem"

Running the risk of repeating myself, the significance of the final solution of the early phases of the innovation process, as described earlier, cannot be underestimated. At the same time, it is of crucial importance that the process – as well as the resources allocated to it – is managed carefully. This might seem like a contradiction. This book is about encouraging allocation of more resources to the early stages of a development project, and yet, on the other hand, a certain degree of providence doesn't hurt either. In general, the process, as we see it in many technical and commercial "cultures," has less focus on the problem identification and framing phase than processes influenced by design thinking. However, my points of view are not unknown, as such. In Jonathan Cagan and Craig M. Vogel's book *Creating Breakthrough Products: Revealing the Secrets that Drive Global Innovation*,[19] which in many ways, builds on the stage-gate principle, focuses much more on the explorative stages. Their process is divided into four stages or rounds: "identifying," "understanding," "conceptualizing," and "realizing" the opportunity, thus actually devoting three out of four stages of the process to what we often refer to as the "front end."

Getting to the End of Round One

Our fifth element of the first round is to choose which problem to actually solve. While in Cooper's model, this is done already at the entry gate – before a project exists, so to speak, this clarification makes up a quite significant part of the model I'm referring to, actually the entire first round – which is actually less than in Cagan's and Vogel's model, where

---

[19]J. Cagan and C.M. Vogel. (2013). *Creating Breakthrough Products: Revealing Revealing the Secrets that Drive Global Innovation* (New York, NY: FT Press).

this part of the process makes up 50 percent of the whole, the two first out of four stages.

Somehow, it would be tempting to use Cagan and Vogel's model as a starting point, and the reason why I still chose to start from Cooper's stage-gate and its many offsprings, it is because it is by far better known than the other, but also because it actually accommodates a classic design process much better. I'll get back to why later.

As of now, we relate to its slightly modified version found at the beginning of this chapter, and according to it, we have reached the second gate – originally entitled "second screen" and often referred to as "project approval" or "interim approval." We are lagging a little behind, as we're still focusing on the problem and now ready to articulate the problem we intend to solve. That could, for example, be that after careful consideration, we want to focus on the physical spaces, and how they are being furnished and equipped at schools and after-school activity facilities on the one hand, and the incentives for young kids to engage in physical activity, on the other. This could be one out of two or three highly relevant challenges we could look at, but the one matching our resources better and a challenge resonating with a majority of stakeholders. So now, we are ready to establish a clear-cut and manageable "project," and thus, also which success indicators to pursue.

Fine-Tuning, Continuous Validation, and Reframing

The next few phases are difficult to distinguish, regardless of which model one tends to prefer, as a certain degree of iteration is inevitable, fine-tuning, validating, or reframing until all vectors point in the same direction, and there is consensus around a reframed and final concept for which problem to solve and by which means. In our example, it means that we have moved from observing a problem – overweight state and obesity in a particular age group – to knowing which situation to address to make the biggest difference to the individuals affected by it.

Reframing and Articulation of a Coherent Concept

In the 1990s, we were all congested by concepts, they were all over the place and meant anything one could imagine, a little like growth and innovation and transformation and flow today. However, the word actually does mean something, and cannot be substituted. It means "a general and unifying idea" for something, which is exactly what it is we need to develop for how to deal with the facilities we offer young kids. If we had known from the beginning that this was what we wanted to look at, we could have discussed solutions with our stakeholders from the outset, but we have invested time and resources to first now – but hopefully with significantly higher precision – being able to describe the project that we're about to embark upon.

This part of the process is all about challenging our assumptions and preconceptions, to validate whether the problem we all thought was the right one actually also is the most sensible one to solve or whether the problem we saw was a problem in itself or rather just a symptom of any number of other problems. And now, we are actually ready to move into a solution mode, as we know exactly which problem it is that we want to focus on. This is where we make sure that we have all the knowledge and user insights that we need, establish the right team with the most relevant competences and experiences, identify which stakeholders to engage throughout the rest of the process, and allocate sufficient resources to work design-methodically also in the next three rounds, allowing for iterations and continuous fine-tuning of elements, means, and success indicators.

Based on our processing of the original scope and the scenarios coming out of the preliminary stages for how to address the problem of overweight and obesity among 10- to 15-year-old kids, we are ready to address the most "significant" problem: the one which we believe that solving might have the greatest effect in the long term and the greatest potential for creating a shift among already affected users.

At this stage, all involved parties hopefully agree that no stones are left unturned, and are all equally enthusiastic about actually solving the identified problem. What happens now is that we are ready to develop a plan for *how* it will be solved. In the making of this plan, we benefit from all the knowledge and user insights that we got already in the first round, and it might not even be necessary to involve stakeholders again. The outcome of this round, after all, is not the solution itself, but a "proof of concept" – a thorough evaluation of whether the chosen solution has the potential to be realized, and whether it will solve the problem to a satisfactory degree. And then, we're ready to head for the next gate.

It seems fair to mention at this stage that proof of concept is used to describe various levels of "proof" – from theoretical models to almost ready for production prototypes. In our case, we use the term to describe a verbal and possibly also visualized concept for a solution, not a close to final and mathematically substantiated model of what our solution is all about. As from now on, referring to our "case" would require much more insight into the user population and how schools and youth facilities are already designed, and as the overall problem of overweight and obesity might possibly be much more effectively addressed by other means, be it what they eat, how social interaction is stimulated, or any other factor, I now leave the age group and specific challenge, before I move onto thinner ice than what good is.

A "proof of concept" can only be signed off by the project owner or whoever has the overall responsibility for the delivery of a solution. To do so, as this person or body has most probably not been intimately involved in the process so far, a relatively precise and unambiguous description of which problem we're setting out to solve, within which economic and human resources and when delivery can be expected are key elements of the project plan. It also needs to describe how available resources will be allocated and prioritized, which resources are available "in-house," and which need to be sourced and procured, how and when stakeholders will be engaged, and how and by whom the project will be managed. It can also include how often and in which format progress reports will be made, how and when the project objectives and progress are communicated externally, and how the final solution will be launched. In principle, there's no limit to what it could include, but as a friendly piece of advice, don't overdo it; hold on to the privilege of allowing changes as you go along to the extent possible. And at any rate, what matters is that whoever has the mandate to do so, says, "OK, guys, here we go."

From Proof-of-Concept to an Actual Project Plan

Let's make a detour from the creative process for just a brief moment or two. Right here, as we now – for the first time – know what it is that we're aiming for, is, as already indicated, where we will benefit a great deal from developing a detailed plan for the remainder of the design process. Now, as we know "grosso modo" what the challenge entails, there is no reason why we shouldn't invest some resources in planning the journey step-by-step, define our success criteria and milestones. In terms of what that means specifically for a design project, the most typical format is what we call a "design brief," a document which serves as a common source of information for internal and external team members, and which, in addition to laying out timelines and resources, also defines the next phases, action by action. There are probably tons of useful templates for a design briefs out there, but in my opinion, a good one also includes a short resume of the process up until now and the background for it, an overall description of how assumptions and limitations with regard to resources, responsibilities, progress, and reporting, but also requirements with regard to preferred competences and methods, internal and external suppliers, and other stakeholder engagements, either preferred or required. This is also where external services are typically procured for the first time, unless external experts have already helped with the framing and stakeholder engagement process. Such external suppliers may include designers or design agencies, strategy and analysis experts, anthropologists and expertise on the specific product, service or activity in question. Help can be requested from NGOs and trade organizations, advisory councils and private sector consultants to identify and choose the most suitable partners and to make sure that the partnership builds on a solid foundation of contracts and expertise.

Before entering into a creative mode, it makes a whole lot of sense to conduct a quick "audit" to make sure that the project is reasonably dimensioned and that it actually supports, unambiguously, the "proof of concept" we have invested so much time and energy in reaching.

Ideation, Stakeholder Iterations, and Prototyping: Toward a Common Point of View

A new project is born – or possibly several, after an unusually long period of labor, some would say – but at least with a clearly articulated goal and with firmly grounded consensus on which means have to be activated to reach it, on which terms, and in collaboration with whom.

We still don't know the solution, although at this point, all involved parties and every single team player will probably have their own qualified propositions as to where it is we're heading. Now, the design process, as most people know it, starts, or the development process or change process – both of which are design processes when it comes to it; so from now on, I will refer to it as the design process.

Other, Already Existing Design Process Models

Just like there is an unknown, however quite significant number of project management processes out there, there is no immediate lack of design process models either. However, just like the first category, design processes also look alike and are very often inspired by and related to each other, and actually quite often to the model that I have chosen as a reference.

In general, design process representations will often be circular, or at least somehow indicate a cyclic and iterative movement back and forth between its individual elements, possibly as a reaction to the very often linear process models deriving from the natural sciences, engineering, or business administration. The most extreme interpretation is probably Damien Newman's "squiggle of the design process," which I mentioned in the preface of this book. Looking at the more "moderate" models, they often seem to converge and overlap with their linear cousins, and many words and terminologies as well as the underlying logics of the models are often the same – all of which is quite natural. Whether one is trained as a designer, economist, or engineer, it makes sense to visualize a certain progress from a starting point, A to Z, an end, or from a clearly defined point of departure, A to B, a future and more attractive situation. As one of the most quoted design theorists, Herbert Simon has contributed to the discussion of what design is: "Everyone designs who devises courses of action aimed at changing existing situations into preferred ones".

Also, my choice of reference model has been taken from a source, pre-viously referred to a few times already, the global design firm IDEO – this time, a model, which was introduced in connection with the opening of d-school, an independent institute at Stanford University in 2004, established by, among others, one of IDEO's founding partners, David Kelley and the founder of the global IT-company, SAP – Hasso Plattner (Figure 3.6).

The reason for my choice is partly because the model – possibly better than any other – by help of its loops visualizes what makes it a design process model and not a stage-gate model, and because IDEO, with all due respect to all other well-known as well as unknown, innovative, and by all means sympathetic design agencies in the world, is the individual design agency which, more than any other, has contributed to move design from the arts and crafts domain and into a process-oriented and ROI-focused reality.

As already mentioned, what characterizes the d-school model are the loops and iterations, which are built into both the process and the DNA of the thinking it represents. The model has a number of qualities and features by which it could replace more traditional development processes. However, as I see it, it has a weakness compared to a stage-gate model in that it lacks the valuable and quite meaningful "feature" that the gates represent – points in the process dedicated to evaluating progress and to either apply the brake or give the green light to embark upon the following stage.

A closer look at the model reveals that it prescribes both reflection and reframing. It starts by understanding the problem and the context it's part of. The next phase is to observe and establish an unequivocal "point of view" – a starting point for ideation and approaches to how to solve the problem. Here, more than in any other phase of the

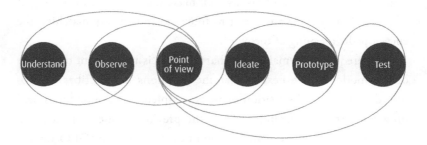

Figure 3.6 The IDEO's process model launched in collaboration with and at the opening of d-school in 2004

process, IDEO has refined brainstorming as a methodical tool, where no idea should be kept from being posted on the wall. After the ideation phase, another well-known design approach, prototyping, starts. A prototype is not necessarily something made at the very end of the process, just before starting production or launch. It is, in principle, just a preliminary representation of a product, service, or activity serving to demonstrate and test ideas and where we're heading at any stage of the development process.

As a matter of fact, prototyping often starts already in the observation phase – even understanding and scoping; at the very front end of the process – simply because designers cannot help themselves. They have, as visual beings, an urge to start sketching and scribbling from the very minute they enter into a conversation or any other situation, and to build small impromptu "prototypes" from paper and chewing gum and saucers and sugar cubes the very minute a coffee break is called. A little further in in the process, when the first really good ideas start resonating around the table, prototyping becomes a formalized part of the process, providing "something" everyone can relate to and discuss as one moves along. It seems quite unique to the design process, as the objective of a prototype is not only to represent "a preliminary version of a product before actual production starts," but to make meaningful propositions for how to deal with a situation more tangible and understandable – to help all involved parties to see the same – thus an invaluable part of the iterative process. And actually, it fits perfectly into a linear process, as a means to make more qualified assessments when arriving at the next gate.

Eventually, as a final solution approaches, the prototypes will have a degree of "readiness" and finish, which make them suitable for testing in whatever context they are meant to function, thus finally matching the encyclopedic meaning of the word.

A prerequisite to make sure that progress is made from one phase of the model to the next is that the iterations it prescribes are observed. When the observation phase is completed, the outcome is held up against the understanding from the previous phase, adjusted and fed into the next phase, entitled "point of view" in the IDEO model, and repeating the same backward loop every time a new milestone has been reached and to make sure to stay on track. As earlier mentioned, the ideation phase – and in particular if undertaken in the IDEO tradition – will produce a wealth of ideas, good, mediocre, and outright lousy. To determine which ideas are pursued, the "point of view" is used as a guide. If an idea, however interesting, does not resonate with this common understanding and reference, it will only create problems at a later stage, interfering with the process of transforming ideas into a solution or solutions. And in exactly the same way, prototypes are discussed, as they become increasingly advanced and realistic representations of possible solutions, in light of whether they support the point of view or not.

A question which will always cause some discussion is when to start the involvement of users and other stakeholders; for example – is it here? And, obviously, they should be involved in this part of the process, as they would most probably have contributed with valuable knowledge already at the two previous stages, and as they will contribute throughout to the end and beyond. However, at the same time as underestimating the value of stakeholder engagement, it is also important to know the limitations of such engagement. Users engage in the process to represent users resembling themselves, just like other stakeholders reflect the desires and preferences of their peers. Thus, granting such "reps" too much influence on the choice between scenarios and prototyped solutions can be dangerous, and increasingly so as the final result approaches and the differences between alternative solutions are increasingly marginal. The further away from the "overall principles" of how to address an issue and the more detailed the questions asked are, the more likely it is that the stakeholder response represent personal views, rather than those of an entire group or population. Moreover, asking stakeholders to make choices between several solutions resembling each other quite often makes their choices rather arbitrary. The researchers Sheena Iyengar from Columbia University and Mark Lepper from Stanford University[20] in a comprehensive study found that there is a direct correlation between the number of alternatives to choose

---

[20]S. Iyengar and M. Lepper. (2010). As referred to in "The Tyranny of Choice - You Choose," *The Economist*, December 16, 2010.

between and the individual's insecurity in the situation where asked to make a choice. This goes for the groceries, where the number of consumers actually choosing an item is higher where the number of alternatives is limited than where it is endless. It also goes for students, spending much more time on deciding which one out of a long list of essays to write, and experiencing much more anxiety and uncertainty doing it, than those students who are asked to choose one out of three. And finally, American consumers having a wide range of pension schemes to choose between more often fail to actually take out a pension than consumers who are presented with a limited number of alternatives. A qualified choice, in other words, requires that the individual is able to understand and assess all available alternatives on an equal basis. If such an overview is perceived as too demanding or time-consuming, the choice made is often arbitrary, which is dangerous, or – even more likely – the individual proves unable to make a choice.

A Few Words on von Hippel's Lead User Model

Another popular reference in the design community is the previously mentioned Lead User Model, developed by Erik von Hippel, and his theory that the most interested and dedicated users are the most valuable experts of whatever challenge we're facing. The thinking assumes that the lead users are users, whose visions of what an ideal solution would be today represent what a broader and more mainstream market will demand months or years from now on. Since lead users already possess often detailed knowledge about something, which for most people belongs to the future, they are valuable "futurists" and forecasters within their specific field of interest. Besides, lead users have often attempted at solving problems or improving on the existing, which means that they might already have developed valuable concepts, which can be fed into the development cycle at a rather early stage (Figure 3.7).

So, the morale is that the users, whether labeled lead users or experts on their own lives, or who from any other background are chosen as stakeholder representatives, will guide and unlock the door to valuable

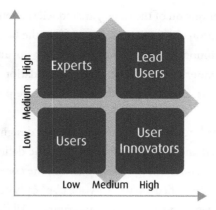

Figure 3.7 von Hippel's Lead User Model, introduced in the article "Lead Users: A Source of Novel Product Concepts," Management Science in 1986.

knowledge, which can inspire progress and possible solutions, but that does not necessarily mean that they are the right ones to ask when making decisive choices. It might sound like a paradox, as that's what we've done for generations in the form of focus groups, who were confronted with an x number of alternatives – from new soda pop flavors to new corporate logotypes. But here, we need to remember that the focus group confrontation was often – more often than not – the first time ever that users or other stakeholders were invited into the process, and alas, all too often, too late.

Giving Form and Shape to the Solution

Even the most hard-headed among us can sometimes get confused by the ambiguity of words we use all the time. Design is one of the richest, measured by meanings and interpretations and by colloquial use. I made up my mind already when starting on this book that I will not open the semantic discussion once again. I need, however – for the sake of understanding the models used – clarify which short and utterly incomplete definition I lean up against; a representation of what a material or immaterial solution will appear, which needs it will fulfill, and how it can be realized.

In the original version of the stage-gate model, the fourth phase covers testing and validation. So does ours, except from the fact that testing has taken place continuously throughout the process up until now, and in particular, throughout the last phase. And the validation, we took care of up-front; in fact, we already know for sure that we're pursuing the right end goal.

Thus, our fourth round is called "detailing and design" – still referring to the already cited and not entirely unproblematic definition. We know that the entire process from beginning to end is one coherent design process, but now, we've reached what "everyone else" calls design; the chosen solution will be given its final form and appearance. All the details and the actual experience of it; the emotional as well as visual and tactile aesthetics of the solution we ask someone to embrace will be worked with in detail.

Just like in the previous chapter, I do not dare indicate what the solution to the overweight and obesity problem would be, but no matter which choices were made, this is where we make sure that the solution appeals to the target group, speaks their language, and resonates with their cultural references, and where we make sure that it is perceived as "cool" or "tight" or "fresh" or whatever, we grown-ups would call attractive, is called in the school-yards nowadays.

Also now, at this quite late and irrevocable stage of the process, we want users and other stakeholders to be part of the process, but not necessarily for the same reasons as earlier. As I will revert to, designers and other experts are likely to be deeply immersed in making sure that their professionalism is given a fair chance, restricted as they have been by stakeholder influence until now, so it needs to be quite explicitly laid out in the project plan how users and others are engaged stage by stage – also here, approaching delivery. If a user or stakeholder centric approach has been chosen from the very offset, there is no plausible reason why this fundamental assumption should suddenly be discarded. If one is not ready to deal with their presence until the bitter end, another strategy should be chosen from the beginning. But again, make sure that they are asked to have an opinion where it matters, and not where it merely reflects their own taste.

The Final Phases

It's a deliberate choice from my side to focus more on the earliest phases of the innovation process, rather than the more operational development phases and implementation. My concern is how we identify the right problem and how we choose among different angles and approaches, which could all, theoretically, create value by being pursued, how we develop possible scenarios through collaborative efforts, and finally, how we formulate the most effective solution to a precisely formulated challenge.

And yet, I will take us through to the end of our process, not to leave it hanging in the air. In the original stage-gate model, this stage is called "launch" – after having passed a gate called "go to launch" – which, as a digression, always reminds me of the signs hanging in shop-windows, on one side saying "open", and on the other, "gone for lunch." Launch is a relevant term when introducing a new product in the marketplace; we know it, for example, from events such as the Apple launches of new or modified product versions. However, as our context could just as well be the rolling out of an organizational change or rebuilding a facility for a public service – or the service itself – or the implementation of any other material or immaterial solution, our last gate is simply called "GO" – as in go or no-go. Hopefully, that is open enough to accommodate the outcome of any development process, from a process in its own right, via business models to new or improved products, services, or activities – or, for that matter, a new app.

In any case, the activity following the "go" in itself ought to be seen as a development process in itself, observing the difference from the third stage, that now, we need to understand a context or market or audience, as opposed to understanding what the problem is. But the principle is the same; a common point of view needs to be established for who this audience is and what it will require of support for it to be adopted. This means new rounds of brainstorming, ideation, and sorting among ideas, prototyping and choice of strategy to ensure uptake, and just as for the development process itself, it is important to engage the right people – experts as well as diverse stakeholders – and to make sure that the significance of, and the time and resources needed to undertake this crucial part of the process is not underestimated.

Merging Two Models into One

I have leaned up against two models until now, Cooper's Stage-Gate model and d-school's design model, as separate and as products originating in two individual and quite different professional disciplines. I have also referred to de Mozota's important work to integrate design as a methodological element within a framework, which is partly inspired by Cooper's model and partly by other management and development theories. I have also mentioned that many corporations have developed their own methods based on some of the same sources, such as LEGO, which is among the largest individual users of design professionals and design services in Scandinavia, working with their own innovation model in parallel with the classical stage-gate model.

Based on my studies of these models and countless examples of how organizations work with design, as well as on my own contribution to developing a design management framework for the public sector, topping more than a decade of working with designers and as part of the international design and innovation community, I have ventured into merging my own interpretation of the two models into one representation, which will hopefully come across as a source of both clarity and new inspiration.

I find it interesting that by scanning the hundreds of development process models you can find by a simple Google search, it is quite easy to determine, just by the look of it, whether it stems from a so-called creative consultancy, such as a design agency or architectural firm, a communication agency, or an agency rooted in the management consulting or engineering industries. Both the visual language used and the terms chosen will very often reveal a model's origin.

Thus, I have made an effort, and choose to see it as a quality in its own right, that my own representation, the INNOLITERACY model, can be traced to and embraces both management theoretical and design empirical elements (Figure 3.8).

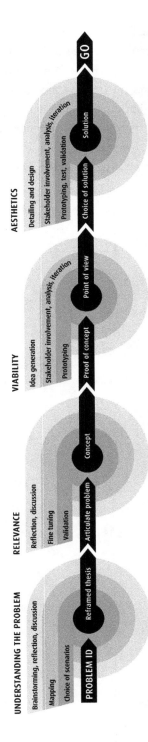

Figure 3.8 The INNOLITERACY model; my own attempt at integrating an iterative development process into a linear project development model, and inspired by a.o. IDEO and Cooper's stage-gate model

The model might, in itself, not be a breakthrough or a game-changer, to the extent that many organizations already work according to it; however, most of them do so unknowingly. What justifies its right to be published is that it structures the iterative processes in a manner which releases the potential of design thinking and methodologies throughout the process, supporting the postulate that it contributes to minimizing risks, and at the same time, fits perfectly well into a linear project management tradition, focusing on progress and meticulous management of time and resources.

PART 4

Innoliteracy – Close-Up

To start with, and before we embark on a detailed close-up of the model, I may need to present the reader to a "disclaimer." In many projects where the task at hand is to develop "another" product or service within an already overcrowded category, a product which the consumer may decide to pick off the shelf or let it be, following what I in an article in 2002 labeled "soap dish design," a term adopted by at least two national newspapers in a number of following articles, a process like the one described might appear as overkill, unless, of course, you want to challenge whether or not to actually develop such "another" one. I guess that the precondition for meaningfully using the INNOLITERACY model as a guide, the project at hand needs to be characterized by a certain degree of complexity.

One Iteration at the Time

While the previous chapter described the iterative stage-gate model in light of the models by which it has been inspired, this chapter will take you through the model, round by round; in part to add some more detail and perspective to the model's individual elements, and also to open up for the design methodical approaches built into it.

First Round – Understanding the Problem

The foregoing gate presumes that a problem has been defined – either a specific and isolated, but more often than not, a complex and multifaceted problem. The process now starts by understanding the problem and its complexity, its character and scope (Figure 4.1).

The core activity of this round is to frame and if needed, and very often the case if done properly, reframe our understanding of the

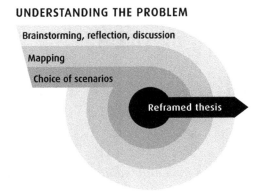

Figure 4.1 The first round of the INNOLITERACY model – from problem identification to a problem thesis

situation at hand. This understanding is achieved by engaging relevant stakeholders in workshops with brainstorming sessions and one-to-one dialogue, supplemented by time and space for both individual and collective reflection among team members. After this round, we will possess a much clearer picture of which elements the problem or challenge consists of and the insights needed to actually articulate one or several challenges that we assess to be significant enough to address, but also to discard those challenges that will have to rest for now.

Brainstorming, Reflection, and Discussion

There are several ways of going about brainstorming, such as IDEO's already mentioned "The Rules of Brainstorming" and Edward de Bono's "Six Thinking Hats." Which approach you choose is not the most important, as is not whether you choose to run one or a series of workshops or brainstorming sessions. It all depends on how many people you intend to involve, the complexity of the situation, and the time and resources available. What is more interesting is the fundamental principles of brainstorming; to ensure an environment of openness and inclusiveness, which inspires all the individuals invited – introverts as well as extroverts – to contribute as much as possible and with what you need to fill in the gaps. Not all people are used to speaking up in crowds, and it is crucial that the session does not become a stage for those who love to hear their own voice. This can be ensured by composing the groups with care and with regard to internal relations between the group members and by facilitating the discussions in ways which gives everyone equal chances to contribute, by being precise when posing questions and by setting up rules for everyone to observe. Equally important is that both overall strategic, political, and intellectually demanding questions as well as operational and tangible experiences are addressed and recorded. Unless already experienced at planning and moderating such sessions, it might be a good idea to hire someone who has specialized in facilitating conversations and in animating maximum engagement by the participants.

Besides the managed and structured part of the process, the brainstorming itself – individual and collective reflections and the conversation that entails – is of equal importance and value. This is often where the most sincere and uninhibited observations are shared. Thus, it is important to see this as a process rather than an event, to make sure that ideas can mature and that the time between the structured sessions can be used constructively. Some people just need time to process and linger, while others are more spontaneous and better at shooting from the hip.

The overriding idea of engaging as many individual resources as possible at this stage is, of course, to be presented to as many angles, experiences and questions as possible, and to make sure that all the individually vested capacity you have actually access to is exploited to its fullest. The outcome from this stage is twofold; on the one hand, it ought to produce a long-list of issues to consider and look into, and on the other, it will anchor the project broadly, ensuring ownership among as many implicated parties as possible.

Mapping

Not all the information needed to make sure that no stone is left unturned is available internally or among close allies, even though their input should not be limited to internal affairs. They may have valuable knowledge of possible conflicts of interest and other show-stoppers, both internally and externally. However, your stakeholders are made up of a wide range of different players. In principle, a stakeholder is any person, group of individuals, organization, company, authority, or other entity, which

Figure 4.2 John M. Bryson's matrix

may have direct or indirect influence on your project, or which may be directly or indirectly afflicted by it. That, of course, sounds massive, and a stakeholder map may also look quite overwhelming, but again, there are tools and methods available to handle this too. One such tool to map and analyze one's stakeholders is Professor John M. Bryson's matrix, in which individual stakeholders are clustered in a diagram, based on their influence on and their own interest in your venture (Figure 4.2).

Depending on where a particular stakeholder or group of stakeholders fits into the matrix, the model offers guidance with regard to how and to which degree this "player" needs to be informed, actively engaged, or monitored, and to which extent there might be possible conflicts of interest one needs to observe. According to R. Edward Freeman, a corporation's stakeholders encompass any group or individual who can affect or is affected by the achievement of the organization's objectives.[1]

The concept of stakeholder engagement does not only encompass users and others who are intimately involved in the process or who have an obvious interest in it. A thorough mapping of interests having a potential impact on an organization's priorities will most often be significantly more comprehensive than what would result from a quick and superficial glance.

Moreover, research by, among others, associate professor at University of Southern Denmark, Alex da Mota Pedrosa[2] shows that a

---

[1]R.E. Freeman. (1984). *A Stakeholder Approach to Strategic Management* (London, UK: Pitman).

[2]A. Pedrosa. (2009). *"Motivating Stakeholders for Co-created Innovation"* Open Source Business Resource, December 2009. http://timreview.ca/article/311

meticulous mapping, analysis, and strategic processing of an organization's stakeholders add value to the organization in four different ways: with regard to the development of new knowledge, the development of new skills, building new relations, and reducing risks. International research within each one of these four areas confirm that this significance is valid across organizational sizes and structures.

In other words, a thorough analysis of which effect a project or a specific solution might have on the world around us is a central part of this stage. Included here – in particular – is the environmental and social impact our project might possibly have.

John Thackara, who is one of the most acknowledged "provocateurs" in the design and innovation community, writes in an article that:

> Design – in general – is subject to a curse by obsolete metrics like quality and performance. Most of what comes out of the endeavours of designers contributes to wasting astronomical amounts of energy and natural resources. Most products, services and systems with adverse effects on our development – including the energy consumption and emissions they entail – would never have existed without the contribution of the creative industries, and designers in particular.[3]

Internally, the same kind of mapping is also important. Besides the aforementioned capitalization on the knowledge already existing in the organization, these internal exercises will also disclose who actually contributes and who possesses the most valuable insights, important criteria for being recruited to the project team, reference groups, or expert panels, thus actively engaged throughout the project, and for some in connection with the assessments taking place in each one of the four gates, in particular.

Choice of Scenarios

The third element of the first round is to organize and process the knowledge gathered in the two preceding "operations" into a limited

---

[3]J. Thackara. (2011). *From an Interview in Inform 1/2011* (Copenhagen: Danish Designers).

number of scenarios – three is a good number – to support the reframed thesis, which is the output and delivery of the first round, and on which the first big decision will be made; consensus on a precisely articulated problem is important because it determines and guides the next rounds of development. A thesis is an assumption and starting point for discussion; in other words, it is not by any means carved in stone, still leaving opportunities to reframe and refine the project matter in the round to come. On the other hand, it serves as an argument to actually define and establish a project and why it makes sense to allocate resources to establish a project team or to commission the necessary expertise to take on the challenge.

The outcome of this first round, thus, is a thesis based on insights and an understanding of the problem at hand – acquired through engagement of all relevant parties, dialogue, and reflection, followed by mapping and processing into a recommendation for which problem or problems to actually address.

Second Round – Relevance

The second round, thus, will be based on the decision made in the second gate, focus on moving from a point, where we all see the same problem to a point, where we, based on the chosen scenarios, agree on a concept for how to address the problem (Figure 4.3).

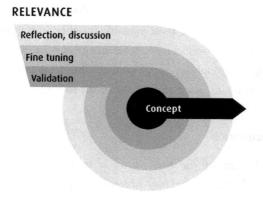

Figure 4.3 The second round of the INNOLITERACY *model – from thesis to proof of concept*

To get to a point where we can deliver a comprehensible concept for how to deal with the articulated problem we all agree on, it's worth taking the time needed to discuss and challenge the problem once more and to make sure that we're actually solving the right problem. It may sound familiar and as a tedious repetition of what we've already done, but it will most probably pay off handsomely in the end. This "right" problem will, after the round, be more facetted, more precisely cut, and angled than what we started with, which was "merely" a validated starting point for articulating a conceptual approach, on which decisions will be made in the third gate.

Fine-Tuning

Needless to say, this round is also based on reflection and discussions on a team basis as well as with individual stakeholders, but it also requires a great deal of desk research and devotion to detail. After the first round, we now need to be more targeted to find out which resources and means need to be allocated to address the problem and which one out of the presented scenarios make the most sense after analyzing costs and benefits and long-term consequences.

To get to such a stage of clarity, we divert from the creative process as we now know it and indulge in data collection and benchmark analysis, calculations and cost benefit assessments, value and risk analyses to qualify each one of the presented scenarios and to add flesh to the bones of the outcome of the previous round.

This stage of the process will most certainly reveal factors which alter and call for reassessment of the thesis we started with. Most probably, one or two scenarios will suddenly appear significantly stronger or weaker than the others as a result of these new insights, perhaps to a degree and with such conviction that we suddenly know for sure which path to choose. Other times, another level of complexity is unveiled, or factors which seemed complex from the start suddenly prove to be of lesser or no significance. The whole exercise aims at disclosing all factors needed for a final test of the project's validity and of the viability of each individual scenario presented.

Validation

More often than not, the test will be passed if you have already invested the amount of time and resources recommended to the front end, but probably in the form and shape of a "problem 2.0" – a revised and refined version of the original problem. This revised version is probably a much better starting point than the first one, but it needs to undergo a last check to ensure coherence with the original analysis and the solidity needed to stand the test in the forthcoming gate, the scrutiny of "proof of concept."

The most significant element of the two first rounds is the idea of repeatedly framing and reframing, as described in the second part of this book, and as a means to do so, individual and collective reflection, as described in the first, applied as a recurring element in a range of methodical processes, leading toward clarity and assurance that we are actually solving the right problem.

Third Round – Viability

After the second round, you have now successfully reached a "proof of concept" – an approach for how to address the challenge in question, which in itself can most probably serve as a brief for the work onward. When choosing the heading "viability" for this round, it is because this is where we find the most viable, the most effective solution, perfectly in line with the principle of "form follows function" (Figure 4.4).

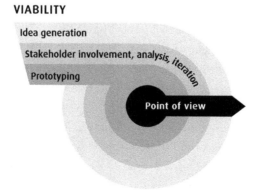

Figure 4.4 The third round of the INNOLITERACY model – from proof of concept to joint point of view

This round, in other words, is all about making a solution work, to codevelop and cocreate together with users and other stakeholders, to prototype, test and analyze ideas and actual solutions in workshops, through role-playing and other qualitative methods. The key at this stage is to create a framework, which as realistically as possible represents the collective "point of view," and inspires the best possible propositions for solutions or for elements which could be part of a solution to the articulated problem.

Idea Generation

Some call it "ideation"; others idea development or idea generation. In any case, the method resembles those applied in earlier phases, such as brainstorming and ideation workshops, however often more targeted, and with a different profile of participants than before. The reason for this is that now, it's not merely a question of generating new ideas as such, but ideas which directly support the concept agreed, and to further develop, cluster, and combine ideas, something that takes both certain skills and a certain degree of experience. The idea generation gradually develops into an iterative process, where ideas are not only developed, but also materialized as prototypes, as tangible as possible, however simple at this stage, to allow testing by and dialogue with users and other stakeholders.

Prototyping

Traditionally, prototyping has been used primarily when developing physical objects and artifacts. There is no reason, however, not to prototype new services, a new procedure or transaction, an environment or an integrated solution, combining any of the above with technologies or digital interfaces, as the fundamental idea is to test the functionality – and functionality only, at this stage, of parts of or an entire solution. As an example, a new service can be prototyped by constructing a number of fictional users – whether clients, patients, or citizens – by help of so-called personas, archetypes described and portrayed in detail. The level of detail of the prototype itself can evolve over the course of a project, from simple sketches in the early phases to life-like representations of a new product or interaction when we approach the crucial time of delivery. In any case, the purpose of it all is to establish a unanimous "point of view," a mandate to finalize the solution in detail.

Point of View

The point of view, as stolen from IDEO, serves the purpose of making the final principal changes to the chosen solution, before an often costly round of making the solution as attractive as possible. This is also the last call to challenge whether the solution responds adequately to the challenge we set out to address. If there are still alternative solutions or versions of a solution on the table, now is the time to make the choice. And yet, we're still discussing the solution in principle, its ability to meet functional demands and perform as required, while the process of styling and making sure that the solution resonates with its audience emotionally is yet to come. So, we're approaching the fourth gate with a solid and viable "point of view" – the best principal solution we've been able to come up with, one that everyone believes in as the one to bring forth to implementation and beyond.

What happens, one might ask, if there is no consensus, or if everyone agrees that "we're not quite there, yet"? Or, even – which happens from time to time – the team is not able to make a choice. If a situation like that incurs, it is crucial that there is a certain contingency in the budget and project plan, so that an extra iteration can be built in; back to "proof of concept," bring in a couple of new "eyes," and go over the alternatives once more before a final choice is made. Pursuing a solution for which there is not full support increases the costlier risk of failure after one has passed this "point of no return," either by someone intervening between now and launch, or by simply experiencing that the doubt was actually a mirror of real reservations in the marketplace or among the users. So, one owes both members of the team and the project owners to keep on developing – not until perfection, if anyone believes that perfection exists, but until all involved parties believe enough in the solution to fight for it and until all indicators point toward success. Because we're now getting awfully close to a point that may incur both financial investments in prototypes and molds and in both individual and collective prestige and reputation.

On the other hand, if the resources and activities prescribed until now have been observed, the likelihood that uncertainties at this stage cannot be overcome is rather slim. The whole idea behind the meticulousness from the very beginning and up until now is to make sure that everyone has the same vision for what the solution is, just like we managed to establish consensus on what the problem was earlier in the process. Very often, when people fail to agree on the solution, it is merely a reflection of the fact that they do not agree on the problem.

Fourth Round – Aesthetics

After having chosen which solution to go for in the fourth gate, the time has come to deal with all the small, yet important details, moving our focus from function to form, to ensure that the solution resonates aesthetically (Figure 4.5).

There is no way around, at this point, to clarify what I mean by aesthetics. For many people and in colloquial use, aesthetics describe the beauty of things, however beauty as perceived and decoded by our eyes. The original Greek word "aisthetike" means "the sensuous." Professor Morten Kyndrup from Aarhus University in Denmark describes it in his book *The Aesthetical Relation* as "something, which exists in the relation between a subject, experiencing and judging something in a particular way and an object, which may be calculated to have an aesthetic effect."[4] Aesthetics, as he understands it is, in other words, a record of how a person as a whole experiences and connects to or establishes a relation to any product or situation, whereas the term has previously predominantly been used in connection to the arts.

While focusing on aesthetics is most certainly a matter of intellectual interest and of delivering an end result of which we can be proud, the most important reason is to ensure that the final solution resonates with and is embraced by its intended users.

---

[4]M. Kyndrup. (2008). *"Den æstetiske relation - Sanseoplevelsen mellem kunst, videnskab og filosofi"* (*The Aesthetical Relation – sensorial experiences between the arts, sciences and philosophy*) (Copenhagen, Denmark: Gyldendal).

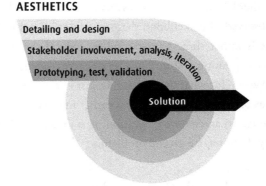

AESTHETICS

Figure 4.5 The fourth round of the INNOLITERACY model – from choice of solution to a final GO

Detailing and Design

Pursuing the logic of "form follows function" – although I do not in any way regard it as a more valid dogma than so many others – we have not really embarked upon the many challenges of understanding what it takes for a solution to resonate aesthetically. Surely, most of the people who have been involved in the process from the beginning have a pretty clear picture on their irises of what a solution should look and feel like; if a physical output, be perceived and related to. However, this too needs to be developed; the solution needs to be given a form or expression, an appeal that that spurs its audience to embrace it and regard it as being attractive – or cool . . .

Stakeholder Engagement, Analysis, Iteration and Prototyping, Test and Validation

As indicated by merging two iterations into one, we fundamentally do in this round as we have done in all the former: we engage users and other stakeholders in the process, we prototype and test, and we make sure that our solution is given a form or expression, which attracts instead of distracts, which appeals rather than appalls. At a stage of the process as late as this, we can, to a certain extent, choose to be more exclusive with regard to when we invite stakeholders in, and how we take advantage of their advice. One opportunity is to invite people who have already been part of the process and use them as a wall against which alternative expressions are played, and then, to catch the feedback and use it as a guide for your choices. Even experts on their own lives are not necessarily experts at typography or colors or patterns, but they respond – as we all do – rather intuitively to sensory stimulation, and being able to record and process such response can be quite valuable. Quite effective tools and methods for doing so have been developed over the last decade or so, and it may be a smart move to engage professionals to actually get the most out of such confrontations.

On the other hand, it seems quite unlikely that a design process such as the one described does not involve professional designers, and more than at any other stage of the process, one can rest assured that the designers will make sure that their influence and contribution is not underestimated. We're now quite clearly maneuvering in a field which has historically been the sovereign domain of design professionals, so with all due respect for user engagement, make sure that you allow those who know their craft to contribute with their expertise, just like we have depended on others' expert knowledge throughout the process.

Solution

The outcome of this round is something resembling, or as a matter of fact, being a final solution, or in some cases – perhaps most – any number of slightly alternative solutions. It may have taken some time, but on the other hand, we now rest quite assured that the solution is a meaningful response to a thoroughly processed and precisely articulated problem, almost no matter which of the alternatives we choose. However, often a choice has to be made. Sometimes, the choice can be to go with five different versions of a product or service, an assortment, while other times, there is no need for or room for more than one ultimate solution. What matters now is that the choice is made with care, whether based on own intuition and intimate knowledge of the audience, or based on metrics and facts and figures, and that all responsible parties rest assured that the journey has ended in the right destination.

The last gate in the INNOLITERACY model – the last decision to be made – is to give the chosen solution a "GO," a green light and a tap on the shoulder. This by no means implies that from now on, the solution should be left to its own devices. There might be several considerations to be made. One should – if not already taken care of at an earlier stage – assess whether the solution in part or as a whole needs to be protected by any available immaterial rights mechanisms. The solution will most probably need to be supported by communication campaigns, a visual identity, and other support relevant for the specific solution may need to be developed, instructions and training might be needed, and so on. However, my recommendation would be that each and every one of these are developed as independent projects and on their own premises, merely entailing a number of new processes, starting with asking the right questions, reflecting, and reframing, just like the solution that they will all proudly support.

A Few More Words on the Five Gates – The Decisions to Be Made as You Go Along

The INNOLITERACY model aims at enabling a combination of cyclic design iteration and the linear processes that many organizations work by, instead of seeing the two approaches as adversaries and as incompatible.

In the walk-through of the process, I have focused, quite deliberately, on the four rounds of iteration, more than on the gates separating them from each other. It is in the fourth round that better products, services, or ways of doing something are conceived, and which are more likely to resonate with an unattended-for need in the marketplace, with a desire or demand in society, or with an aspiration to cater for a more sustainable and resilient future. And yet, it would seem wrong to totally disregard the decisions, which need to be made as the project progresses. Partly, the model calls for a different set of decisions than many other processes do, and partly, some of the decisions you may already be accustomed to making will have to be made at other points of time than what you would otherwise do in a pure-bred stage-gate model.

Provided a project is developed in strict accordance with our model, five instrumental decisions have to be made.

Problem Identification

If we look closely, and if identifying problem is a goal in itself, we can find problems anywhere and anytime. Using "problem identification" thus is not a matter of finding as many problems as possible, but of identifying the most relevant or most serious problem at hand and one in which investments to address the problem makes sense, whether regarded through corporate or societal lenses. Identifying a problem does not require or imply that we know anything about what needs to be done, what needs to be changed, or developed. It merely means that we have a vision for which outcome we desire – whether measured in market shares or revenue, or in desired BMI for 10- to 15-year-old kids.

Articulate Problem

The difference between this gate and the former is that we have moved from acknowledging which overall problem it is that we want to address, to being able to articulate which problem we intend to solve. If that sounds like gibberish, there's not so much more to say than; I really tried. The foregoing chapter tries to explain the rationale behind each one of the two decisions, but just to exemplify, if the problem identified in the first gate is falling market shares (and where the reason for opening up the gate is a need to recover market shares), the problem in this gate may be narrowed down to whether the falling market shares are caused by the wrong assortment or product mix, by an unfavorable price-quality ratio or by old-fashioned packaging design or point-of-sales material, thus guiding us to which problem to actually solve. And, while the parallel problem with overweight 10- to 15-year-olds is a statistically measurable matter in the first gate, the problem in this gate has been boiled down to resulting from either malnutrition or lack of physical activity or after-school facilities or lack of meaningful dialogue with parents or any combination of the above.

Proof of Concept

This decision is perhaps the most important one, in the sense that this is where the original thesis has been challenged, facts and figures collected and processed, and stakeholders drenched of insight and relevant knowledge. This is where the green light is given to start a development process or not, which would most often just mean that the project team will have to go back and recalculate and dig up some more facts and figures or re-frame the concept to make it more credible or understandable or sharper, whatever the reason for rejection at the gate proved to be.

Choice of Solution

This gate is somewhat self-explanatory; this is where the solution to the problem is chosen – in principle and based on whether it functions or deliv-ers the effect needed, not based on what it looks or feels, or how it is pre-sented to the user. The actual "styling" of the solution comes next, so all we can do is to assess the solution, based on the facts recorded and observations made, as to whether it corresponds to the "point of view" that we all agreed to earlier. The importance of this decision should not be underestimated, as it also constitutes a de facto point of no return with regard to what it is that we want the solution to do for us. From here on, provided green light is given, the only thing that remains is to make sure that the solution is given an appeal and appearance, which resonates with its audience.

GO

Having failed to find other words, which seem to work transversally across products, services, procedures, and environments in all sectors and regard-less of size and complexity of the project itself, the last gate is all about giving the solution a final GO. At this stage, the decision is made on the basis of a true representation of what the solution is, what it looks like, or how it feels or appears, down to the smallest detail. Hence, a GO is not only a mandate to roll out or push the button or launch or release, it is also an acknowledgement that the identified problem has been addressed in a manner in which everyone believes. In most cases, it also means that we are prepared to take on the new processes it entails – alongside and in support of implementation of the solution as such. These may be indi-vidual design projects in their own right, and are often crucial elements in making sure that the solution actually fosters success, whether measured in higher market shares or lower BMI.

Quite often, and in particular, in projects of a certain magnitude such as a new nationwide public service or a new banking service scheme or a flagship store or service center, it would make sense to implement the solution as a "pilot" to start with. By establishing one or a limited number of pilot projects in full scale and fully operational, but in controlled and monitored environments and for a limited period of time, needs for minor adjustments as well as both positive and negative user experiences can be recorded. This allows for an extra round of optimization before the next 50 or 100 facilities are rolled out. In the example of the flagship store, it can be a rather banal observation, such as the cash register being placed in a fashion, which requires an extra and perhaps uncomfortable movement by the employee, thus influencing negatively on the quality of the transaction, and in the example of the service center, an observation may show that by lowering the counter by a few inches, the perceived experience is improved on both sides of it. The costs, however, of this extra round and of recording and of adapting the solution to take such real-life insights into consideration is marginal compared to making the adjustments in a hundred different locations. We know the principle from website development, where a "beta-version" will always be tested by an invited audience before the final version is uploaded.

Time and Money

No two processes are identical, thus every single development process will be experienced as unique to the challenge at hand – its complexity and extent, and to the project team and stakeholders involved. For the same reason, it is impossible to prescribe how much time and which resources are needed to undertake the process. The most effective way of finding out is to start by drafting the process according to the model already being used in your organization, and then, challenge each individual part of the process in light of the INNOLITERACY model and the project at hand. The better you know your own process, the easier it will be to assess which changes are needed to take on some inspiration from this book. Thus, it is not only a recipe for a successful development process. It can also be used as a checklist from stage to stage as you progress through your own project and process to assess where and how it would enhance and which consequences it would have in terms of calculating extra or saved time and resources, internal as well as external (Figure 4.6).

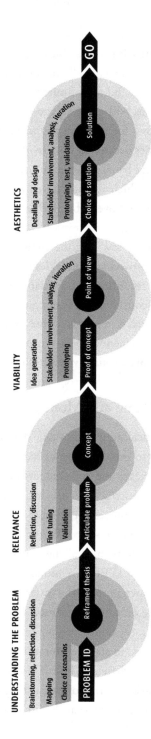

Figure 4.6 *The INNOLITERACY model*

Checklist

It is allowed to be inspired, and thankfully, also to apply the knowledge and insights that others have spent years, perhaps a lifetime, to acquire. Instead of reframing my own model into a checklist, which would probably come across as a third – and even more tedious than the second – repetition of the model itself, I have chosen to edit and reframe a checklist found in the previously mentioned book on design management by Brigitte Borja de Mozota. In the book, she refers to three levels of design management: operational, functional, and strategic. I choose to see the three levels as symbiotic in my own model, and therefore, find it natural to merge the most significant elements from her three checklists into an overview of which decisions have to be made as a direct consequence of choosing to work with design as a methodological starting point.[5] The following list is my own compilation of essential elements to be aware of, however inspired by the more elaborate checklists found in her book.

Define target: Define qualitative targets for every single touchpoint: products, services, communication and physical environments – depending on the objectives and activities described in the mission, and evaluate the direct correlation between the use of design and user experience.

Prepare: Allocate resources to develop thorough and precise design briefs, identify internal and external stakeholders, possible conflicts of interest and the potential of each staff member to engage actively in the design process.

Coordinate: Coordinate the project and the activities entailing from the design process with day-to-day activities, other ongoing development projects, action plans, and overriding strategies.

Adapt: Adapt the scope and size of the development process to match the resources and complexity, as well as other ongoing activities in

---

[5]B. Borja de Mozota. (2003) *"Design Management – Using Design to Build Brand Value and Corporate Innovation": pp. 213 (Operational Design Management Checklist), 236–237 (Functional Design Management Checklist) and 255–256 (Strategic Design Management Checklist)* (New York, NY: Allworth Press).

the organization to ensure that all members of the organization support and embrace the project.

Embed: Spend some resources on explaining the correlation between the use of design methods and existing targets for quality and innovation, and make sure that all parts of the organization understand that they also have a role in ensuring the success of the project. Encourage cross-disciplinary relations and tasks between product development, business development, design, marketing, and new technologies.

Anchor externally: Communicate new design projects and solutions to external stakeholders and invite them to be part of the project through social networks as well as actual engagement processes. Establish relations to design schools and universities when embarking upon the development of new ideas and concepts.

Anchor in top management: Make sure that the senior management of your organization understands and endorses the use of design methodologies and tools, and allocate an active role for them in the process, wherever their input can benefit the project and wherever such engagement could further their understanding of design thinking.

Source smartly: Define exactly which skills and competences you need to successfully undertake each phase of the project and balance the benefits of using in-house and external resources, both of design and of any other skills or competence needed to support the process.

Manage: Develop KPI's and detailed budgets for each phase of the design process to enhance both the planning phases, but also audits and evaluations. Allocate resources realistically – divided on internal and external resources, materials prototypes, and communication – and do not underestimate the time a design process takes.

Monitor: Establish a protocol for monitoring the process, focusing on decision-making gates, progress and efficiency, and benchmark these with previous design projects as well as other processes undertaken in the organization.

Disclaimer

A process like the one described is probably idealized and more exhaustive than what one would see in real life – just like most other recipes. They work as intended under optimal conditions and will always need to be subjected to scrutiny and common sense and to be adapted to the individual situation. I want the INNOLITERACY model – just like Cooper's and IDEO's – to be regarded as a valuable source of inspiration and as a guide to how design might fit into your specific process.

It also needs to be said that numerous highly successful companies and organizations represent both creative cultures and design-driven solutions – without working as prescribed by IDEO or by anything resembling the process I suggest. Lots of organizations have either tried and rejected, or never even tried, collaborative methods based on user engagement; even iconic design-driven companies such as Apple or "typical" design product suppliers such as Alessi or BODUM. They work in radically different ways. The Italian professor Roberto Verganti[6] challenges the overwhelming focus on user-driven or user-centered innovation. His thesis is that radical innovation can never originate from user-driven processes, and that such innovation can only be driven by technology and the designer themselves. They define a product's meaning, thus also new standards for products and services within any given category. He does, though, acknowledge the role of user engagement when it comes to incrementally improving on existing products and services.

This is just to acknowledge that we discuss a field of many variables and opinions, and of professional and academic discourse. I hope that this book will be received as another qualified and valuable, however by no means conclusive proposition for how to work with change and innovation, or as I choose to regard it – for how to find the right solution to the right problem.

---

[6]R. Verganti. (2009). *Design-Driven Innovation – Changing the Rules of Competition by Radically Innovating What Things Mean* (Boston, MA: Harvard Business Press).

PART 5

Risk: To Seek, Manage, Minimize, or Avoid Risks

There is a Norwegian animation movie from the 1970s, called "The Pinchcliff Grand Prix," boasting as one of its main characters the eternal pessimist, Ludvig. He has a standard response to virtually all situations he encounters: "Det er farli', det . . ." – which translates directly into "That must be dangerous, I'd say . . . ." Lots of people are Ludvigs, rarely contributing to improvements or change, and most certainly not to anything resembling breakthrough innovation. Innovation, in itself, is not necessarily risky business, but one has to be open to enter into unknown territory if innovative solutions are one's objective.

We all run risks every single day – all day – even while at sleep and not actively doing anything risk-invoking, there is a certain risk that something unfortunate will happen. Obviously, and as a rule of thumb, there is a correlation between one's actions and the choices we make on the one hand, and the extent to which we expose ourselves to risks, both as private individuals and our choice of relations, activities, and the challenges we pursue in our daily lives. We also run risks as part of a community, where decisions are made as a group, whether that group is one's own family or friends, the football team, or local constituency. And we run risks in our professional lives, whether employee without formal influence, as part of a team, or as someone with a dedicated management role. Regardless of our position, the extent to which we tend to perceive something as dangerous or risky depends on a number of factors: one's personality, previous experiences with running risks, and not least, depending on which consequences, running risks and then failure entails.

Regardless of whether we discuss risk taking in a private or professional context, the amount of risks taken, and the consequences our risk taking potentially imply, depends on the choices we make and the decisions we make or have influence on. Some people seek risks as a source of energy, however more often seen in people's private rather than their professional lives, ranging from extreme sports via gambling – beyond the weekly lotto coupon – to more colorful and outright unmentionable activities jeopardizing long-lasting relations. Others see dangers everywhere and build their lives on a narrative, which neither encourages "unnecessary" risk taking nor exposes them to situations, where risk taking is an option. To a great extent, we manage the degree to which we want to be exposed to risks and the nature and magnitude of the risks we take. For the same reason, the concept of risk is given quite a lot of attention, both as a theoretical field, and not least, as a deadly serious field of professional focus, often referred to as risk management.

In principle, risk management is a professional discipline devoted to identify, assess, and prioritize real or potential risks. A crucial element of risk management is being able to forecast what may possibly go wrong, a prerequisite to the subsequent elements of assessment and prioritization.

Another term which I'd rather prefer that we do not dwell on, as I see it as the enemy of all things good, is risk aversion – the endeavors to avoid risks of any kind and for any price. When I have to deal with it, however briefly, it is simply because a great number of organizations both in the private, and perhaps in particular in the public sector, practice it big-scale. They often invest more resources in making sure that nothing can possibly go wrong than in creating better and more meaningful solutions to problems, which could actually and sometimes easily be solved. However, all development processes incur an element of risk. Often, that risk is limited to the new development not actually solving the problem at stake, leaving the ROI on level zero or negative, corresponding to the cost invested in the venture. Other times, the risk can be significantly higher than "merely" having wasted the resources invested in the project itself, and such projects in particular require a prudent and professional way of managing such risks. But the solution is never to let the risks stand in the way of needed change and improvements, renewal, and innovation.

For some, it may appear almost meaningless to lecture the leaders of today or tomorrow on risk management. After all, it is possibly the most significant individual factor determining which decisions are made across sectors and industries, and unfortunately, the management part of it often tends to be practiced as aversion. Sometimes, I sense a great deal of suppressed fear of taking risks, even among the most conscious and reflected leaders, most probably because the concept of fear, and admitting to it rarely is seen as a career booster.

But it's there, and it's a dominant factor influencing the choices and decisions of many leaders. And, it has its price. Fear prohibits many organizations at attracting competences and profiles, which do not resemble or even duplicate those they have in advance, because how should they go about making sure that they get the most out of a staff member whose competences are different than one's own, and whose contribution they do not fully understand? Fear prohibits organizations at innovating; at embarking on projects which could ensure competitiveness and relevance in a changing market, out of fear of not succeeding. What if we fail? What if we waste our shareholders' money? What if we just stay clear of risking anything instead? As an anecdote, some years ago, I decided to take a 3-day course at project management, offered by a leading provider of post-educational courses, now part of the international group Mannaz; somewhat paradoxically the Old Norse word for "human being." The by far most significant focus over the 3 days was devoted to risk management, to working with mathematical models and variables, costs of time units, and other metrics. To me, it came as a surprise, as I never really considered the risk as a critical factor in the projects I managed. While I always thought, as well as practiced by the principle that project management was all about motivating people to work together, somewhat naïvely, I learned – inspired by a "you win some, you lose some" attitude – that project management more or less equalled risk management, with or without contingency for what former vice president Al Gore always added, "and then there's that little-known third category." That's just not how things are done any longer, which is probably good for all, as long as risks are managed sensibly, but when risk is managed in a manner which discourages, or even suffocates the energy and courage needed to foster innovation, and which encourages the fear of failure to win over and over again, it is a losing game not only for the organization, but for society at large.

What might be even worse than a conservative, but honest attitude toward risk management when new paths are being trod is the constant emergence of new phenomena – often in disguise as being progressive – are new approaches to minimizing risks disguised as novel concepts of governance or compliance. My postulate would be that many companies' investments in and flagging of CSR (Corporate Social Responsibility) in reality are purebred risk management measures. Instead of being "outed" as an organization without soul and heart and consideration for those in need or for the local community, or simply to comply with legislative demands or industry standards, prescribing social responsibility to be accounted for in annual reports, it seems like a sound investment to support a worthy cause – just in case. None of that, in my opinion has very much to do with responsibility. If it's all a question of not breaking the law, "Corporate Social Liability" would be more precise and much more overtly a risk management measure. I'm often thinking about what the world would look like if we called things by their rightly deserved names, but that, I guess, could fill an entire book on its own.

The bottom line, unfortunately, seems to be that what, more than any other individual factor, drives decisions in both the private and the public sector is avoiding and managing unavoidable risk.

> In the increasingly emotional and regulated business environment, effective risk and opportunity management has become a basic necessity for every organization, as has the ability to communicate effectively with external stakeholders about risk. The potential costs of poor communication with stakeholders during this process are enormous but the potential benefits of effective consultation are even greater.[1]

One of the most effective forms of risk management is to listen to and benefit from the insights of trusted employees and colleagues, engage

---

[1] M. Loosemore. and F.T.T. Phua. (2010). *"Stakeholder Engagement in Managing Risk"* Proceedings of the 18th CIB World Building Congress.

users and other stakeholders in meaningful dialogue, and to listen to one's own common sense and intuition – take time for reflection and processing of the information harvested, and make the decision you, as a trusted and responsible leader, have to make. Which, in a way, is the process that I have taken you through, step by step, supplemented by the necessary competences and external expertise, an approach that research over the last couple of decades has documented as being the most effective both to foster innovation and to minimize risks.

A Few Cases from the Real World

An overriding ambition with this book is to cast some light over the correlation between reflection, reframing, and risk reduction. One way of doing so is to present – however briefly – some "real-life" examples of how the choice of process and methodology, emphasizing the stakeholder engagement components, on the one hand, and the project outcome on the other.

Some years back, while the ideas of collaborative processes, cocreation, and stakeholder engagement were still young, the Danish government granted a substantial amount of money over a 4-year period, dedicated to an initiative called "Programme for User Driven Innovation." Consortia consisting of organizations, universities, and companies could apply for funds from the program to undertake development and demonstration projects focusing on the then rather novel and politically captivating concepts of user-driven and user-centered innovation. One of the projects in which I had the pleasure to partake – DESINOVA – was a collaboration between the Danish Chamber of Commerce, Danish Designers, and a university innovation unit. Moreover, a dozen independent designers, design agencies, and innovation professionals were actively engaged in the project, which focused on applying and further developing the said methods to foster innovation in service-providing companies – from insurance companies and pension funds to private hospitals and retail operations.

The companies came with an assignment, or rather, a problem they wanted to see solved, and the idea of the project was to address the problem with other means and methods than what the company itself would otherwise have done. This is, and ought to be, a principle for public funding of development projects – a so-called market failure – to avoid unfair competition and to make sure that new knowledge is actually generated.

In several of the "cases" worked with over the course of the 2 years that the project lasted, applying a user-centered approach revealed quite early on in the project that the challenge raised – the "thesis" – was misconceived, and that other, unrecognized factors were much more instrumental to what was seen as a problem. One of the "testimonials" captured after the project had ended was from a senior director of a large Danish pension fund. He admitted that the most important and highly valuable learning on their side was to invest much more patiently in identifying what the real problem is. Until then, they had worked with user engagement in the form of focus groups and other means of user confrontation to validate new product ideas, but now, it seemed obvious that the users needed to be engaged from the very outset of the project to help prioritize which initiatives to take. Adding to that, they bluntly admitted that they did not have enough knowledge and understanding of especially young people and of their motives and needs in relation to take out a private pension.

A nation-wide retail chain within home electronics had also identified a problem; they hadn't been able to attract female customers to their outlets. However, they also had a clear-cut idea of the reason for it – being their inability to attract female staff with whom female customers could identify. So, the problem they wanted solved was how to attract female staff. However, by challenging the thesis and by engaging both male and female customers as well as existing staff members and group management in a re-framing process, it proved that it had nothing to do with the gender of staff members. In fact, most female customers actually preferred being advised by a male member of staff, as their general perception was that men know more about technical issues and electronic product information. The problem was actually much simpler than originally perceived; female customers simply did not feel attracted by the extremely product-focused environment, exclusively focusing on the newest technologies and bits and bytes and technical specifications – not on the most important buying criteria among female customers: energy consumption, the user experience, and how the product would fit into their home environments. They simply just wanted more attractive outlets, which made them feel welcome instead of alienated, and some guidance resonating with their criteria for purchase – not from a staff member, but through better shop layout and atmosphere, signage, and product presentation. Then, after having taken the first moves on their own, they were more than happy to be served by a male member of staff.

Moving beyond the confines of my own home turf, Denmark, there are oceans of good cases underpinning the sensibility of investing in the front end, in the very early phases of a development process. One such case is the development of London's Heathrow Terminal 5. The renowned design management specialist, Raymond Turner was responsible for design development, just as he was for Heathrow Express and numerous complex infrastructure design projects. He has also advised a number of global companies on their strategic use of design. In his recent book, *Design Leadership – Securing the Strategic Value of Design,*[2] he writes that the reason for the massive investment, both financially and in terms of time, in a creative explorative process before actually commencing on the actual planning of the terminal building, was a great deal of focus on and consciousness of how to understand and manage the risk factors of the project. He says that "the risk of creating the wrong solution and for the long-term cost of making the wrong choices were at least as important for our early stage assessments as was the ambition of creating the optimal solution." Hence, the development was organized according to an entirely new principle, spread out on three equally important teams: one for incoming passengers, one for outgoing passengers, and on for transfers. And instead of defining the project as "designing a new airport terminal," it was defined as designing "the world's most refreshing interchange" – regardless of whether that transfer was from one aircraft to another, from train, bus, or car to catch a flight or from arrival by aircraft to onwards transport by train, bus, or car. Because that's what an airport is for – to facilitate an interchange.

By adopting such a mind-set, the project owner, British Airport Authorities, realized that they had been frighteningly close to making the wrong decision, to embarking upon the wrong project – a multibillion pound investment, without strengthening Heathrow's position as an

---

[2]R. Turner. (2013). *Design Leadership – Securing the future of Design* (London, UK: Ashgate).

interchange. They might have increased the flow of passengers by a couple of million passengers a year, but neither its owner, BAA nor its largest user, British Airways, would have been able to use it as an argument to fly via London instead of via Frankfurt or Schiphol or Paris de Gaulle, because the only thing that matters in the airport industry, at the end of the day, is the traveler's experience – something which is monitored and measured almost day by day, an entire industry whose competitiveness is entirely based on one thing: the differences between excellent, good, mediocre, and lousy design.

For a couple of decades, now, an interesting concept has attracted quite some attention – globally, and in the United States in particular: the concept of "family-centered care." The background for it is quite simple. In pursuit of a more effective hospital sector, and after having wrung the effects possible out of medical staff, nurses, and caretakers, one started looking at whether some of the more banal operations performed by staff could actually be performed by family members and other visitors instead. The list of such activities grew quite long, but it didn't really help, as the real problem was that visitors stayed for as short as possible. There were no facilities making it possible to combine a visit to the hospital with the pursuit of other activities, such as working, and the atmosphere did not invite longer stays, where the visitor could read a book or see a movie. In fact, the hospital was not a very attractive place to spend time at all. However, dialogue with family members showed quite a few would actually spend substantial time with their sick family member, if only such facilities existed. By taking the consequence of these new insights, and in close dialogue with user representatives, the wards were furnished with comfortable chairs for reclining, a more homely atmosphere, and an actual work station, as well as better catering facilities, internet connections, and whatever else it took for family members to feel comfortable. As an immediate response, family members and friends stayed for hours and whole days with their loved ones instead of the mandatory 15 minutes, automatically taking on chores such as fetching a glass of water, accompanying the patient to the restroom, and fluffing the pillow – and even more importantly, just being good company for the patient, which in itself can have a significant therapeutic effect. And just as immediately, the same chores were removed from the to-do list of staff members, who had suddenly more time to cater for those who didn't benefit from family and friends, and to allocate more time for professional care and nursing. In some cases, capacity has been released to an extent, which allows for more flexible working hours and engaging in development work, instead of constantly being stressed by lagging behind. An unexpected effect has proved to be of even greater importance, as patients are, in average, being dismissed earlier than before – in part explained by the more inspiring and healing atmosphere, and in part by the attention from and help by their peers.

Juncture

So far, so good – you may think. It all seems wonderful that organizations solve their problems successfully with the help of reflection and applying design thinking and methodologies to make sure that they solve the right problem. But what exactly does that have to do with risk management?

The greatest risk of all those an organization can run into is that its investments are not sufficiently capitalized, eroding long-term ROI and solidity, which in turn, is the fastest route into marginalization and eventually closure. Unless, of course, and hopefully in due time, the management is changed as is the direction.

The greatest risk of all those a public sector can run into is to manage our joint resources in a manner which turns civic society against the system, questioning the competencies and priorities of its leadership, and whether the ratio between taxes paid and benefits returned is reasonable. A long time ago, it didn't really matter – the public sector was a protected reserve – but today, the consequences increasingly resemble those that we know from the private sector: changes in management, with or without golden parachutes, and new directives from the political environment, the public sector parallel to the executive board.

The risk of the pension fund was that it could have wasted substantial amounts on a campaign directed at young people without actually understanding the background for their tepid interest in their products, unless the senior management had discovered the value of engaging their audience at a very early stage; by engaging them in the development of the products themselves, rather than just trying to understand what kind of advertising young people respond to. In any case, no matter how successful the campaign would be, the effect would most probably be limited if the product itself were not perceived as relevant.

The risk of the home electronics retailers would be to hire female staff, thus challenging their strong position vis-à-vis their core target group, men, while the wanted effect of attracting and communicating better with female customers most probably would have been slim or nonexistent.

The risk that the growing gap between the perceived patient experience and available resources would increase stress symptoms and sick leave among hospital staff was a decisive factor for why American health care professionals in the 1990s started focusing on family and peers as a resource. Interestingly enough, the significant results recorded in the United States over two decades do not seem to have impressed their European colleagues. Searching for knowledge about family-centered care or healing reveals only few signs of interest in its potential. I was able to find only few signs of interest in the concept in Europe, and what I found seemed to focus on trends for treating alcoholism-related mental illnesses, referring to the importance of engaging family members actively in the therapy. Perhaps Europe is losing out on a massive, however complex and challenging potential for increased effectiveness as well as enhanced user experiences.

Having both the obligation to, but also the privilege to make decisions on the behalf of others entails a great deal of responsibility, but alas, also great risks. This probably explains the conservatism seen in many strategies, corporate as well as of public sector origin. The problem is only that by being overly conservative and prudent, and by averting risks for any price, new risks emerge by themselves – risks of often much greater potential impact.

When recruiting new staff, the prevailing criteria are certificates and metrics. Why? Obviously, they are important sources of information about a candidate, but the underlying reason is clearly that if someone is hired and proves not to fit in, nobody wants to run the risk of being confronted with an "of course it couldn't work, we could have told you – he didn't even have a certificate." Along the same lines, we tend to hire people who resemble ourselves, as hiring someone whose competences we do not understand fully is perceived as risky. How do we know whether we get value for money . . .? The result, of course, is an endless row of homogenous professional environments, where the lack of diversity in itself may prove to be the largest singular barrier for innovation to happen.

We apply the same risk avert "logics" when choosing suppliers; we choose well reputed and well-established advertising agencies and suppliers of copy paper and catering, just to be "on the safe side." And among them, price takes over as the most common decisive factor. The result is that we become stale and complacent, and we lose touch with the novel and invigorating thoughts, and of losing out on creative, often better and probably cheaper solutions than the current, a high price to pay for lack of courage and of the fear of being challenged. To be constantly challenged, also through our choice of staff members, suppliers, and partners, even clients, is in itself a fantastic opportunity for reframing the way we see ourselves as an organization.

Risk is, as previously mentioned, closely linked to responsibility, and I do not for 1 second underestimate the significance of the fact that acting responsibly often entails a certain degree of conservatism. This is only natural, and in particular, where much is at stage, then certificates and documented metric can be decisive, and reasonably so. On the other hand, though, I would claim that most organizations cheat themselves of both valuable competences and of the opportunity of being perceived as an attractive employer by focusing more on avoiding risks than on working with risk as a resource and a natural ingredient of being a dynamic outfit.

Adopting a more dynamic approach on the one hand implies that one has to take more risks than many organizations do today, but it also means that one learns to work methodically with assessing risks and opportunities and to turn risks into opportunities; risks, which are inevitable, and which are often overlooked if not embraced and related to in a proactive manner.

Every time a new process is started, there is a certain risk of failure; whether failure means that the product or service never reaches the marketplace, perhaps it cannot be produced at a competitive price or because the need in the market has been misread or misinterpreted, or perhaps it does reach the market, but will enter the annals of veritable flops. Most companies defend such failures by documenting their processes and project management procedures, including risk management calculations, and their staff members' formal competencies. Actually, and quite thought-provokingly, many companies have a certain percentage of failed development activities written into their strategies and budgets, often based on statistics showing that 20 to 30 percent of all products and services launched in some categories, and up to 80 to 90 percent in others, such as groceries, fail to capture a reasonable market share, thus disappear from the shelves within the first year of existence.

Which, one may argue, is managing risks realistically, but perhaps not in the most constructive way possible.

What if we took another approach and said,

> let's raise the bar from the beginning – allow some more ambition, paired with some more space for play and frivolity when embarking in new projects. And, what if we made our own lives more interesting by hiring more diversely and by adding more angles and perspectives on what we do and how we improve, without giving up on structured and well-managed processes, making sure that we sort the good ideas from the bad as early as possible, that we exploit the often tacit knowledge that we have access to among staff members, partners and suppliers, customers and passers-by.

That would be a much more effective way of ensuring that the products and services in which we invest our heart-blood, as well as substantial amounts of money to develop, quite actually resonate with the marketplace. And it would be a much more constructive approach to working with risk management, and with improving the bottom-line.

The logics are simple, as seen by a simple mind like mine. By investing more in the early phases of the development process, one ensures that the problem is the most relevant to solve; some would call it the most fiercely burning platform. By working with stakeholder engagement, iterations, and development cycles, systematically through one phase of the development process at the time, one opens up for more angles and more experiences, adding precision to the analysis. By engaging users and other experts on their own lives to the extent possible, you create ownership and access knowledge, which would otherwise have remained tacit, and by working with gradually more advanced prototypes throughout the process, the chances of naughty surprises at the costly end of the process – or even worse – after the product or service has been launched, are reduced to a minimum. And at the end of the day, we minimize the risks of burdening both the marketplace and the environment with product and services, which are fundamentally superfluous or obsolete.

A final example could be a publically funded web universe, which was developed and launched in 2010, aiming at raising the interest in reading among younger kids. Since then, it has primarily collected dust – just like books not being read. Kids, it appears, don't really use it – as was the intention, simply because it doesn't appeal to them and is perceived as less user-friendly and accessible than other, commercial sites, and in particular than the social media they use. As a group of librarians from a municipal children's library writes in a blog posting at their own organization's website, "The question is whether the web platform in its current format is the solution. Despite a quite long introductory period, we do not encounter any enthusiasm among the kids." Why is that so, would be my first question. Perhaps one explanation could be lack of engagement of the users – the kids themselves – in the development process. It has primarily been made by librarians and web developers, and by an otherwise fantastic and well-known comic illustrator. So, you may say OK, you win some, you lose some, and no big harm has been done, just because a website doesn't work as intended. And no – no big harm has been done, except wasting an initial investment of one and a half million euros, and an annual cost of keeping it alive at almost half of that. Obviously, the funding has been granted after careful consideration and on the assumption that it would encourage the desire to read among 8- to 12-year-olds, and facilitate their access to quality children's literature. The risk from the very beginning was that it wouldn't be used, and I'm quite certain that that risk must have been acknowledged from the start. Today, we see that the risk was real, but it could have been managed quite differently by focusing on, understanding, and engaging the users from early on in the process, so that the understanding the right problem would had guided the developers to the right solution. Kids want access to the knowledge and inspiration they search where they are already, and they are present at social media platforms, at the platforms, where they play computer games and on the platforms they use while doing their homework. They don't want more platforms or new accesses; they want to find what they're looking for or be triggered by provocations where they already meet virtually. I am quite convinced that more than three million euros until now could have been used more wisely, and I'm convinced that the user could have contributed to it, instead of using a quite substantial sum, after all, on something, which might end up as more of an embarrassment than a modern approach to cultural policy implementation.

There are countless examples of investments in products and services, which never responded to a real need, and the quite arbitrarily chosen specimens above are by no means there to mock or ridicule anyone.

These examples are a rather random selection that I have come across either as a team member, an observer, or as consumer of the daily news, and are exclusively illustrative of situations where I believe that a design methodological approach and a reallocation of resources to the very early phases either would have – or actually did – contribute to a better end result.

Epilogue

This book has been work in progress for years, but it also wraps up two decades of experience and reflections, countless discussions with colleagues in Denmark and abroad, and my very own points of view, which have been either sharpened or moderated as I slowly challenged my own knowledge of innovation processes. Many people have contributed greatly to the confidence needed to embark upon writing a book. I want to mention a few, and in particular, my colleagues at the European project European House of Design Management, a project with a slightly different focus than my book, but which builds upon the same understanding of design thinking. Perhaps without knowing it, Floor Herman, Andy Cripps, and Michael Thomson have been instrumental to the final result. So have three design professionals in Denmark – all with different approaches to the material, but with deep knowledge of design and innovation – by taking time to read and comment on the first draft of the book. It wouldn't have been the same without invaluable input from Judi Olsen, Steen Jauer, and Karen Blincoe. Moreover, I want to mention DJØF's chief consultant, Carsten Nielsen[1], who acted as a coeditor of the original, Danish edition of the book, thus saving me from building barriers instead of building bridges to some of the audiences the book was written for.

Finally, it only remains to hope that the INNOLITERACY model – and the insights and experiences it derives from – can act as an inspiration for decision makers with responsibility for the development of new (or improvement of already existing) products or services, processes, business models, or communication. User and other stakeholder engagement, co-creation, user-centered innovation, and service design are all slowly becoming well-known and well-tested approaches. The challenge that I have reacted to, reflected, and now acted upon is that there still seem to remain a number of barriers for lifting it all up onto a strategy level, where applying it becomes the rule, rather than the exception.

---

[1] DJØF is the Danish Association of Economic, Legal and Political Science Professionals

INNOLITERACY is a proposal for how that can be done and what it would take for an organization to truly embrace and benefit from it, and even more importantly, what it would offer in terms of better results for the individual company or organization, and for all those for whom the products or services of those companies or organizations are of great importance.

Index

OTHER TITLES IN OUR PORTFOLIO AND PROJECT MANAGEMENT COLLECTION

Timothy J. Kloppenborg, *Editor*

- *Improving Executive Sponsorship of Projects: A Holistic Approach* by Dawne Chandler and Payson Hall
- *Co-Create: Harnessing the Human Element in Project Management* by Steve Martin
- *Financing and Managing Projects, Volume I: A Guide for Executives and Professionals* by Nand L. Dhameja, Ashok Panjwani, and Vijay Aggarwal
- *Financing and Managing Projects, Volume II: A Guide for Executives and Professionals* by Nand L. Dhameja, Ashok Panjwani, and Vijay Aggarwal
- *Agile Management: The Fast and Flexible Approach to Continuous Improvement and Innovation in Organizations* by Mike Hoogveld
- *A Practical Guide for Holistic Project Management* by Lex van der Heijden
- *Project Management and Leadership Challenges-Volume I: Applying Project Management Principles for Organizational Transformation* by M. Aslam Mirza

Announcing the Business Expert Press Digital Library

Concise e-books business students need for classroom and research

This book can also be purchased in an e-book collection by your library as

- a one-time purchase,
- that is owned forever,
- allows for simultaneous readers,
- has no restrictions on printing, and
- can be downloaded as PDFs from within the library community.

Our digital library collections are a great solution to beat the rising cost of textbooks. E-books can be loaded into their course management systems or onto students' e-book readers. The **Business Expert Press** digital libraries are very affordable, with no obligation to buy in future years. For more information, please visit **www.businessexpertpress.com/librarians**. To set up a trial in the United States, please email **sales@businessexpertpress.com**.